There Are

No Horseshoes

In Heaven

Carole Herder

For speaking and bulk purchase inquiries:

info@cavallo-inc.com

1-877-818-0037
www.cavallo-inc.com.

Interior Design: Abigail M Copyediting:
abigail.copyeditor@gmail.com

Project Management and Cover Design: The Solution Machine:
www.TheSolutionMachine.com

The events, people and places mentioned in this book are based on fact. While some names and dates are true, other names and identifying details have been changed to protect the privacy of individuals.

Printed in the United States of America.

First Printing, 2015

There are
No Horseshoes
in
Heaven

Carole Herder

DEDICATION

I dedicate this book to my husband, Greg, who saw the courage in me that I couldn't see myself. He was a mirror for me that reflected a stronger, smarter and more fearless and thoughtful version than I could have imagined. His faith in me gave me faith in myself, and through this I overcame the demons and fears that had kept me down. I learned to trust myself. And I came to terms with the ability to walk my talk. I even learned to love public speaking, which once terrified me.

This book is also meant for you if you have ever needed a little courage and a little trust to move forward into your truly authentic self. If you wish to morph yourself into whom you would like to be, I hope this book gives you inspiration. Show up for yourself, your animals, and the people around you. Believe me, if I can do it, you can.

FREE BONUSES!

Send an email to Bonuses@CaroleHerder.com, and you will receive immediate and exclusive access to these great interviews and webinars:

HOOF HEALTH: FACT VS FICTION

Dr. Tomas Teskey explains his purpose of Veterinary Oath and his theories on natural hoof care.   Gain a better understanding of hoof function through his easy-going nature and clear, concise delivery, supported by graphic illustrations.

WHY HORSES CAN'T GO BAREFOOT

Dr. Tomas Teskey delivers an in-depth look at overall horse physiology. Learn horse care requirements from a physical and psychological standpoint, including dentistry and its effect on hoofs.

CAROLE'S "FIRESIDE CHAT" WITH MONTY ROBERTS

Monty's 80 years on the planet embraces extensive travel, interesting relationships and unwavering commitment to improve the lives of horses and humans. This webinar will leave you uplifted and inspired.

Just send an email to Bonuses@CaroleHerder.com to receive instant access!

CONTENTS

1

DATE WITH DESTINY

Gazing into those infinite watery pools, the depth appears unfathomably endless. Yet, why do I sense sadness? Why, in the glassy reflection of chocolate and coffee, is there blackness of pain? Sharply peaked eyelids ramp over the dark beauty of my horse's bulbous globes. Veiled under lustrous lashes, Rocky's eyes portray the intensity of his pain. It beckons me in, summoning me to find out why, in this seemingly normal animal, the windows of his soul are fraught with aching fear.

My first horse, my first love, "Rocky" was in pain and was calling me to assemble my resources and rally to his aid. Looking into his amazing eyes, I realized I had a mission to find out how to help him. My love for this horse propelled me to find resources and solutions—*to help him*.

But even as I knew Rocky needed my help, I wished I could turn away. I sensed that following the path to help him could be insurmountable. In choosing to help him, I would embark on a journey that would change my personal and professional life. I did not yet know what the journey would include, but I knew it would be challenging. I would question traditional practices. I would make enemies, place myself in peril and be ridiculed and challenged. Ostracized from many peers in the horse community, I would be forced to go on alone.

The moment when I looked deeply into Rocky's eyes was as profound as any I had experienced. Uncomfortable as it was, I knew I was face-to-face with my destiny. I would help him. I would find out why he was hurting, and then I would change it. Trusting that I could unearth an ally or two along the way, I began the journey to help Rocky and other horses return to a natural and pain-free state.

CAROLE HERDER

The Call of the Horses

> "Horses make a landscape look beautiful."
>
> - Alice Walker

When looking at my horses in the mix of the lavish summer landscape and late afternoon sun, it is challenging to determine the difference between them and surrounding trees. They stand so still, like inanimate objects. The only movement is the air traveling through their nostrils, filling their lungs and leaving again as they stand there, an extended part of the environment that surrounds them. Wind currents change, and in a blink of an eye they are thundering off, snorting and bucking. And again that flush envelops me—a crazy delight that overcomes me whenever I watch them run. This time as I watch, I feel a tinge of sadness. I am increasingly aware that our society is not shifting and progressing in their favor; their world is becoming vulnerable as our world focuses on horsepower of a different sort

Most kids are not attracted to riding a real horse. Many kids will never even get close to one. Computers are the draw. The speed of technology is more compelling than a meander through a mountain trail on horseback. Housing developments gobble up the pastures like blight pulls down a garden of ripening tomatoes, and fast food parking lots cover land where hay fields once flourished. Horses' natural habitat is diminishing.

Horses are nature-personified, gently moving through the environment like a light breeze that cools you off on a hot day. Then in a second, they exude tremendous power, whipping into a strong, forceful beast that can take off into flight at 40 miles per hour.

I am drawn to watch these splendid animals' movements, the ebbs and flows as they play their various melodies, always in harmony with nature. Sometimes as they move, if I close my eyes a little and just drift, I can see the current-like waves of the ocean flowing across their body as their muscles ripple in motion. They charge across the field in a fury with the force of a tsunami, yet rest and gaze as still as a serene, glassed pond. This dichotomy of nature's gentle influence is to be revered in the majesty that is equus.

Started Young

I didn't grow up with horses, but I had a taste of what it was to love horses one day when I was eight years old. The truth of my heart came with the beating of a horse's hooves. On this special day, I became connected to a horse. Only later would I realize how pivotal this chance encounter with this animal would be to my personal and work life.

That particular day, my family and I traveled down a gravel road in a sky blue '59 Chevy. It was the kind of day when every sense seemed enhanced—the sweet smells of spring and freshly cut grass drifted through the open window of the car; the wind blew softly, rippling the poplar leaves with rustling new growth. Out of the corner of my eye, I saw him—a beautiful, strong, majestic and shiny horse. The wind caught his mane, lifting it skywards as if he had wings.

"Stop the car!" I screamed. Alarmed, my dad slammed on the brakes. We came screeching to a halt—black rubber burned tracks on the hot country road. I scrambled out of the car and ran to the fence.

The majestic beast flew to the rusted wire that separated us and came to a thundering halt. He was shaking, snorting and stamping his right leg. His nostrils were flaring fire-red and wide. I remember every detail. It was as if he was daring me to jump the fence and catch him; it felt as if he were challenging me to come into his world. As I stared at him, my body began to tingle, and a warm flush enveloped me. Bumps erupted on my arms which looked like chicken skin. I felt the warm sweetness of his breath; he was as pure and raw as nature itself.

In that moment I knew my destiny would include horses. It wasn't a matter of if or even how; at eight years old I just knew that my life would somehow include horses.

During our Sunday family dinner later that day, all I could talk about was this amazing beast, how fast he ran, how beautiful, smart, magnificent and compelling he was. As everyone's eyes glazed over after hearing the story yet again, my grandmother (my Oma), took me aside. Dressed in her flowery-printed house dress, she lifted me effortlessly, sat me down on her strong thighs and gave me a bear hug so fierce I couldn't help but snuggle into it—even though I knew I was much too old for this molly-coddling.

"Your purpose in life is preordained," she told me. "Don't ever doubt yourself." And as often could be expected, Oma's eyes filled with lustrous, sparkling tears when she spoke in her most serious, devout Lutheran manner. Her words of encouragement were a German phrase, which loosely translated means "God is guiding you, and all you have to do is listen and love."

They were comforting words, and I never forgot them. I now understand what she meant and how her prophecy has manifested in my life. My love of horses has given me the strength to walk this path, to be the impetus of change, to devote my life with a strong belief for the good of horses, and that, in turn, creates a meaningful life that nurtures me and provides for my family.

Working with Horses

Since the day that I heard my grandmother announce my life's mission, I have been very fortunate to not only make horses part of my life but to do something I strongly believe will help horses. My life's work is to change the way we manage our horses' health. I never really had a choice.

It was not that I one day decided to develop a new product and devote my life to it. It just happened, because once I made some elemental, yet critical discoveries, there was no turning back. The path was laid out in front of me. I am not saying it was easy; it was not always a clear path with obvious action steps. At times I had no idea what was to come next. It was just there, like the yellow brick road—appearing and taking me where I needed to go when it was time for the next step.

Your Journey Through This Book

My intent is to share my journey with you in this book. I hope to provide information about the health and well-being of your horse. My stories and findings may be very different from some other ways of thinking, and I hope you can make the changes required to help those in your care live a longer, happier, more natural life.

And when I say "those in your care," I mean you, too. Often, we care for ourselves last when so many other lives depend on our care. But, in fact, we must be strong, healthy, happy and sound, or we have a lot less to offer to those (animal and human) around us.

Read on to discover more about the science of hoof care, how you can nourish the horse's (and your own) mind and body, how passé ways of thinking have impacted our horses, and how the philosophies of empowerment and independence with a healthy dose of curiosity move us forward into interesting new times.

2

I WAS READY

Long before I owned my first horse, I dreamed and hoped for a horse. I knew that one day, somehow, I would make horses a part of my life. When it was time, it happened quite naturally. Events unfolded and what I, at the time, judged as a bad experience became my hope and excitement for an utterly new life.

In 1993, I was living in Vancouver and had a promising business designing and producing children's clothes. I was thrilled because I had just managed to get this little clothing line, labeled Tadpole, into the department stores, Nordstrom and Saks Fifth Avenue. This felt like the big time to me. I employed home sewers in Vancouver, and I regularly traveled to Europe to bring back beautiful fabrics. Then I would attend trade shows and knock on doors to sell the stuff. All the children I knew, including my own, became models. The fashion photo shoots were a hoot, and the models were always rewarded with yummy ice cream and fun treats. It was fulfilling; I thought I had it made.

Time for Change

Unfortunately, entering the U.S. market was a very briefly held proud feather in my cap. Along came the North American Free Trade Agreement, which completely wiped out my business. Almost overnight, it was impossible to carry on with my business because our domestic clothing manufacturers began production in Mexico, and other clothes were being made so much cheaper that I simply could not compete. I sold off all my stock and closed my business, accompanied by feelings of disappointment and failure.

I had no idea what to do next. I spent some time soul searching, and my thoughts always veered toward horses. I thought of Oma and how she had advised me to follow my heart. What could that mean?

Although I had always enjoyed studying natural remedies and healthy living, yoga, natural foods and holistic medicine, my deep, soul-searching thoughts consistently turned to horses.

I thought of Oma's words and could only think of horses. Horses. My new direction must have to be something to do with horses. When I thought about where I loved to be, it was with nature—outside, countrysides, fresh air, clean water.

As early as thirteen years old, I was an alternative thinker, perhaps as a typical teen, thinking I could change the world. I took issue with the way our society treated everything from pollution to pharmaceuticals. Why just treat the symptoms and not go in for the cure?

And now, faced with change and needing to turn my life in a new direction, I didn't know how to incorporate all my passions. Confused again, I wondered how in the world could I incorporate all these interests into one meaningful life?

Moving to the Country

Jumping into the fire, I decided almost overnight that I must follow this dream and move to the country for a fresh start. Good friends of mine, whom I respected, had moved to the Sunshine Coast in British Columbia, Canada, and I made the fortuitous choice to buy some acreage and move my family there, too. The idea of moving to the country was very profound for me. It was like one of those visions that you can't imagine ever becoming reality. And then, as it recurs more often, it begins to form a life of its own.

My mind's images took the form of sparkling, sun-kissed grassy pastures, frolicking horses, piercing stars in the blackest night skies, and crisp, fresh morning dew with sounds of whinnies echoing in the still air. As I imagined running my fingertips gently over my horses' foreheads and down to those baby bum soft pink nostrils, I could almost feel their warm pulse. I'd have a paint horse and a buckskin. I'd have a quarter horse and a thoroughbred. Oh, man, I'd have horses!

My eldest son, Garret, was six, and Eali, only three months old when we moved out of the city and into country life—the country life that would change everything and chart me firmly on the undeniable path paved of passion but fraught with challenge.

I am sure that on some level my boys understood that I finally had the courage and the resources to pursue my love affair with horses. And they were excited. They were full of life, rambunctious boys, tossing and rolling into our new life with all the vigor of new adventure.

I was 33 years old, born and bred a city girl when I took the big leap. As a city girl, I had never ridden a horse before, but the allure was just too much for me to deny. I attended a local horse show in my new little seaside village on the Pacific coast. I zeroed in on the most popular trainer and boldly approached her. She was dressed in tight Wranglers, with a big belt buckle. Without hesitation I asked, "Will you teach me to ride?" Her clear, blue eyes focused on me, and we stood gazing, as if recognizing a friend after years apart.

"Oh, sure," she said. "If you are up for some fun give me a call. Or just ask around. Everybody knows where I live."

First Lessons

On the first free morning after our move, I got my boys settled in and busy and headed out to Karen's place. I inhaled the heavenly-rich, sweet aroma of alfalfa as we stomped into the barn aisle. There, I was greeted by my date with destiny—horses! They were tossing their heads, snorting and stamping; their coats were a rainbow of horse colors: iridescent white, sorrel, rich brown, glistening black. A group just rode in from a ride, sleek with sweat and huffing hot breath. I knew in that moment I was on the threshold of the new world that would frame my life's journey.

Karen's face was lined and tanned from working outside with horses. Her features crackled like worn leather every time she laughed. A charming character—she told funny jokes and great stories. Her husband, Don, a farrier, was quite the opposite; his conversation only included a series of grunts and demands. They had a typical barn following, an established practice and a full list of clients and horses.

Looking back on that first horse experience, it wasn't the most natural approach to horse keeping. The conditions and approach to horses were not only far from ideal; some verged on abusive. There were 22 horses on 2.5 acres. They were all stalled, all blanketed, they had limited turn-out, they were fed 100% alfalfa hay, fabricated grains, wormers, inoculations, and the lot was besot with a variety of twitchy behaviors—cribbing, stomping, sweet itch, etc.

The horses' discomfort was manifesting in a variety of different ways. I felt sad seeing these horses pent up and so close together. It seemed a far cry from a horse running wild in nature. It was so different from my first, memorable encounter with the mahogany horse who claimed my attention on that dusty, dirt road many years ago. But then, without much confidence, and as it was my first time entering the horse-training world, I just thought this was the normal way of life for kept animals.

Thoughtful Questions

Karen and Don humored me at the start of my questioning. "Isn't she sweet? So curious, so green," they must have thought. But when they realized my inquiries would not subside and that, in fact, many questions were valid in both thoughtfulness and intention, our friendly working relationship took a turn, and I was ostracized as an upstart, troublemaker, and definite "weirdo."

I genuinely wanted to understand why these horses seemed so uncomfortable all the time. I thought a lot about the history of horses and how long they've been on the Earth. I began to wonder, "What is the difference between wild horses and these obviously very domestic ones? Well, maybe it's the fact that we put saddles on them and ride them. And maybe it's the fact that these saddles are rigid and hard and unforgiving—and uncaring, we plunk them on top of their backs."

Back in the Work Saddle

These questions and thoughts prompted me to think about what I could do to help. With my background in manufacturing and design, I began to test out therapeutic saddle pads. My new horse life was beginning to merge with my business life. I received some amazing assistance along the way. These pads really made the horses feel more comfortable. I began travelling to horse shows—first around the province, then around the neighboring province, then throughout the country, and then the neighboring country.

It was a very long journey to where I am now. Today, I am an international speaker and educator, and I am the President of Cavallo Horse & Rider Inc. I'm not only selling saddle pads, but also a line of hoof boots, all available in 29 countries around the world.

We are challenging a 1,500-year-old tradition. A tradition that was forged into the heart and soul of horse owners and their farriers from what seems like the beginning of time. We are challenging it, and we are winning— because it is the right thing. It is the proper thing, and it is the best way to ensure the health and comfort of the horses we love.

It wasn't easy. I was ridiculed, teased and ostracized along the way. I questioned myself and thought of giving up, yet I knew in my heart that I was doing what needed to be done for the horses. I was speaking up for them. If I didn't do it, who would?

3

ROCKY WAS A DANGEROUS BOY

Rocky was my first horse, my first horsey love affair. He taught me to do what I love to do today. Rocky loved to barrel race at top speed in a cloverleaf pattern, and if we were going to be together, I darn well better learn to stay on his back. It was scary, fun and exhilarating, and that was just the beginning. Nothing is a one hundred percent guarantee with horses, but if you are like me and really want to do everything in your power to make sure your horse has the best chance for health and happiness, I will tell you what I learned the hard way, and I'll tell you what nobody wanted to hear. It all started with Rocky.

I had Rocky for about a month when I recognized that he suffered from a high level of discomfort. One day he'd be OK, and then another day he'd be stomping, kicking or agitated. His ears would be pinned back, making him look mean and nasty. It seemed like the only time he was really comfortable was when he was running flat out. I later discovered that when he was running, he had enough adrenaline and endorphins in his system that he couldn't feel the problems that were brewing inside his body. No wonder he loved to run, but it made him dangerous, actually. He was not a beginner's horse. This horse was agitated, and there was no messing around; if I was to survive at all, I had to learn to ride. Right away.

I was very worried about Rocky, but other people kept telling me to stop worrying, get used to it, and just ride. Part of me wanted to listen to them. After all, they had a lot more experience with horses than I did. Maybe they were right. I wanted to believe that everything was OK, that I could stop worrying and just enjoy riding. If I had looked away then, life would have been extraordinarily different.

At first, I thought maybe these "problems" were just Rocky being bad. Maybe it was because of my inexperience with horses; maybe if I learned to be a better rider and trainer the problems would evaporate.

I was very determined. So I trained with top trainers and read all the books, but that didn't seem to help Rocky's agitation. In reality, horses are very willing and able—unless they're suffering significant discomfort. I realized that Rocky needed more than just better training or more guidance.

Rocky, on a camping trip, nearly dumped me in a river.

I started to examine some of the things that we do to horses. I started looking at horses' backs and the fact that many saddles don't fit properly. Surely, that was a departure from the natural lives of wild horses, and an ill-fitting saddle couldn't be good for the horse.

Again, my barn mates thought I was being overly fussy and maybe even scared to ride. "Just ride," they'd say. "Your horse is fine. You're just scared."

It was true. I was afraid of Rocky. He was so troubled that the only time he seemed happy was when he was running off, and that made him a horse to be afraid of. It was like he was running away from the pain. Even so, our temperaments were well matched in a fiery way. We were bonded with one another, and I cared about him deeply.

I'd ask my barn mates, "Well, what about the fact that he felt lame yesterday?" And it wasn't just Rocky. All around me, I saw horses that seemed agitated or sore. Maybe just mildly, but I could tell. They'd limp a little. They'd have swollen legs or discolored hair follicles or other problems.

My barn mates didn't want to talk about it. Whenever I asked these questions, they would tell me, "That's just part and parcel of horse ownership. Get used to it."

I heard this phrase again and again until it came to haunt me. I'm not the type of person to accept things just because someone says it's so, especially if I sense on a deep, intuitive level that something is wrong. My barn mates' answers didn't satisfy me, and I kept questioning. I noticed that horses don't like being cooped up in their stalls all the time, so I started pushing for my horse to be turned out.

"Can Rocky go out?"

"Well, no, he can't, and neither can the other horses" was the standard answer I got. My popularity decreased even more. I was gaining a reputation as an upstart and troublemaker, but what could I do?

> "I don't want to believe. I want to know."
>
> -Carl Sagan

My questions about the practices at that barn got to be too much, and I finally moved Rocky to a different barn. I took him to a much nicer place, where I'd have control over what was happening. In the new barn, he could be turned out and fed what I wanted to feed him. My goal was to provide a better and more natural life for Rocky.

Then something terrible happened. After about three days in the new barn, he came out of his stall head-bobbing lame. Rocky could barely walk.

The veterinarian came in, and he was explicit about the number of problems that Rocky had. He told me they were pretty much insurmountable. He had ringbone, sidebone, splints, and arthritis.

As it turned out, unbeknownst to me, speculation was that the old barn had been feeding him a pretty healthy dose of Phenylbutazone every day, and the "Bute" had taken quite a significant toll on his internal organs. There was nothing to be done. Rocky was going to die. I could barely choke out my gratitude when this kind veterinarian offered to take him to his own barn to live out the rest of his days. That way, the vet could administer the painkillers and manage the symptomatic problems that the painkillers were causing. (It turned out Rocky also had bleeding ulcers from all the drugs.)

So I conceded. With the knowledge I had then, there was nothing else to do. You don't know what *you don't know*. Dr. Keohane took Rocky, and he said he'd allow his son to ride him from time to time to help keep him moving. Dr. K. was very compassionate; he had seen this scenario many times before and understood what I was going through. It wasn't long after, maybe three months later, that I got the call that Rocky had to be put down.

That was the saddest day of my life. Rocky was my first horse, my first love.

But what was I told then? It just happens to horses. That's just the way it is—I should move on. Do you know how they all knew? Because it was happening to their horses, too.

All I had wanted to do was to help Rocky. I couldn't help him in time, but I knew I needed to keep searching. I had to help the other horses that had experienced this same treatment.

4

ASBADASMYDAD

My barn mates were right about one thing: This is the way it is. And if we do nothing, it will always be this way. Our horses will continue having these problems. Then, at age twelve or so, they get diagnosed with navicular disease and bar shoes are applied, or they have a bout of laminitis or colic. We're told to give them stall rest, or we change the feed program or the farrier. The symptoms abate for a while, but if we don't address the reason for the problem, the symptoms just become more severe as time marches on.

Does this sound familiar to you? Have you ever wondered about all these ailments? Have you ever wondered how in the world horses ever managed to survive in the wild?

I have learned firsthand that a bleak scenario is no longer necessary as part of horse ownership. It doesn't have to be that way. We can pay attention to these persistent symptoms and question the reasons behind them. Out of love for our horses, we can be proactive and look for better ways to treat them. I am not saying nothing bad ever happens to horses, but the idea that bad things are just inevitable is ridiculous.

I went on to own several more horses after Rocky, and each time a problem arose, someone would say, "That just happens to horses."

I heard this again and again, but rather than just being sad and accepting, I became more convinced about Rocky's purpose. He came into my life for a reason—to help me change what's going on in the horse community.

Although I didn't realize it at the time, it was there where my personal story really began and over time culminated into my biggest concern for horses' survival—the treatment of their feet.

I do not agree that nailing metal into horses' hooves serves them well. In fact, their feet have gotten progressively more compromised as we continue to view this practice as the most appropriate treatment for their hooves. We have been nailing metal shoes into their feet for about 1500 years. It is now time to exercise our options and make the switch to a more natural practice. It's time to leave your horses barefoot and natural (as they are designed) in their living environment. We know they can handle it because they have been on the planet barefoot for so long.

Here's what I suggest: Have your horse on a barefoot program and simply slip on hoof boots (such as those from Cavallo) when you ride. Horses are survivors, and the structure of their feet has indeed served them well. Why does man wish to improve on God's amazing design? In this book, I will show you how to establish a successful barefoot program, a healthy holistic way of being for your animals and yourself, a new way of looking at your own and your animals' health.

AsBadAsMyDad

After Rocky had died, I knew I wanted to get another horse. The horses I got were beautiful, but the problems still appeared in a variety of forms that I wasn't willing to accept. So this time, I paid a lot of attention to breeding. I thought that might be part of the problem, so I gathered all the resources I possibly could and started hunting for a really well-bred horse.

In the province of Alberta, I found a stunning, well-bred filly. Her nickname was Dorothy, after the breeder's mother. I call her Dot. Her daddy was a champion stallion called *NoMoreMisterNiceGuy*, and her registered name is *AsBadAsMyDad*. She comes from a lineage of competitive winners. These horses are bred to compete and triumph, and even as a three-year-old she was victorious at the Canadian Supreme, a cutting horse championship. Young, strong, healthy, and beautiful, Dot had it all. She was everything I could have ever asked for in a horse

I brought her home and started training her to barrel race. She was fabulous. She learned very quickly, and boy, could she go! She was agile and willing and smart. On most days, we both loved it.

But as I got to know her, what do you think I started to notice? Sometimes, when I'd approach her with the saddle, she'd run away. Other days, she'd be willing. Some days, she'd have swelling in her legs or heat emanating somewhere, or she seemed like she had a hitch in her shoulder. Some days, she couldn't make the turn as easily or couldn't pick up a lead.

I did everything I could to find out what the problem was, not just because this horse was an amazing horse, but because I now really needed to know. This mission was increasing in intensity. I radiographed, and I called in body workers. Up until now, I assumed the underlying problems were related to breeding, so I had invested a lot of money in a well-bred horse. Dot had excellent breeding and outstanding conformation. Yet, here she was with the same problems I had experienced before.

I still had no answers, but I was determined to find out what was going on. I wasn't about to let this horse go down the same path as Rocky and others.

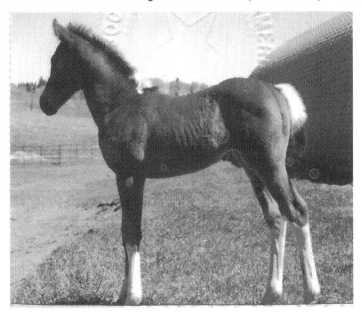

Baby Dot

I continued studying horses and comparing wild horses with our domesticated horses—how they live and how they work. Wild horses don't seem to have all these problems, so what is the difference between our horses and the wild horses that survive and thrive under much harsher conditions?

Signs of Soreness

With Dot, one day a fetlock would be swollen, or she'd be limping slightly or tossing her head. A few days later she'd be stiff and have trouble picking up the proper lead. Sometimes days would go by and she'd continue to exhibit subtle signs of soreness. Many people would look at these signs and say, "Well, that's just part n' parcel of horse ownership—she'll come good." Not me though; at that point in my life, after having lost a horse to health issues, I wasn't willing to accept that this young, perfect, well-bred horse was going to go down that same path.

Need Answers Now

I needed answers, and I needed them now. I was willing to invest whatever was needed to get those answers, to give her the best chance for a complete recovery and get her back to one hundred percent good health. I didn't realize it then, but Dot's feet were the origin of it all, in part because she was shod too early and worked too hard too soon, but moreover because of our commonly accepted practices.

All of the efforts I put forth didn't work. The massages, if they made a difference, were a short-term fix. The radiographs were inconclusive. Of course, I tried my therapeutic saddle pads, which helped, but the issues continued. It was frustrating and made no sense at all. Something wasn't right.

I wasn't willing to simply sit there and just accept what was happening. Instead, I became committed to finding a solution to the problems that these horses kept having. I wasn't going along with the nonsense that health issues are simply part of owning a horse, or that they just needed some stall rest, some Bute, a new feed program or a new farrier.

I wasn't having any of that!

"I'm going to challenge this," I vowed. My passion for horses was going to take me down whatever path was necessary to find out what the real problem was with these good friends of mine.

Now I was compelled to fully and absolutely immerse myself in research. Finally, I had an epiphany that maybe it wasn't the horses, but rather, perhaps it was us, mankind, who is responsible for the majority of these problems that our horses were having.

Could it be? After all, equus has been roaming our planet for 55 million years. If they have design flaws, how could they have survived this long? All these issues that horses are developing with their feet and legs—could it be because we started nailing metal shoes to the bottom of their feet 1,500 years ago?

We've got wild mustangs in the U.S. and the brumbies in Australia running wild all over the place without any metal shoes. Horses worked on farms barefoot. They battled barefoot. Natives rode them barefoot! It wasn't adding up for me. Something just wasn't right.

Those thoughts kept racing through my mind. I realized that if nothing else, metal shoes do absolutely nothing to absorb shock. "Can you even fathom what that must be like for your horse?" a fellow rider asked me one day. I could. All I had to do was imagine what it would be like to go jogging with metal nailed into my soles. I imagined what all that pounding would do to my feet, my legs, my hips, and the cartilage in my bones, my muscles, tendons, and ligaments.

No wonder my horse had discomfort. Metal shoes were nailed to the bottom of her feet, mangling her from the inside out. Forget that! I know that is the standard, and we're all told that they must be used to "protect" their feet, but I had had enough of that nonsense.

No way was my beautiful girl going to continue to suffer. I called my farrier and asked him to come to my house immediately. When he arrived, I explained to him what I wanted to do. Very politely, he told me that I was making a big mistake. He said that my horse's current condition was nothing out of the ordinary, and that all she needed was a little rest or a little painkiller medication, and she'd be back in action on the barrel racing circuit in no time.

I didn't give in. I didn't waver in my decision even though this man was somebody whom I considered to be a close friend because of his kind attention to my horses. Instead, I simply told him that I wanted my horse to go barefoot for at least six to eight months to see how it would impact her health, and that if her health problems didn't improve, I would go back to having her shod.

He didn't argue with me. He couldn't argue with me. He simply did what I asked him to do. After all, this was my horse. I was calling the shots. I finally took control.

When the shoes were removed, her feet were tender and inflamed. I gave her adequate amounts of MSM (sulfur) to help blood circulation. I knew she needed to keep moving, so I hand walked her up and down the road. At the beginning, I considered hoof boots, but back then the styles available were so fraught with problems that I didn't want to deal with them. I also worried that they could potentially do more harm than good. To stay on, they had clamps that seemed to dig into live tissue, so I really couldn't justify using those. I had a trusted vet watching over her the whole time. She was in good hands.

5

BOLDLY TO BIRMINGHAM

The epiphany about the perils of nailing metal into her feet came just as I was about to hop on a plane over to Birmingham, England to attend the British Equestrian Trade Association (B.E.T.A.), which at that time was the largest equestrian trade show in the world.

While there, I met some fascinating people, among them an Australian by the name of Greg Giles. Greg was there to launch a new hoof boot. We chatted about horses and their persistent health issues. I shared with Greg everything I'd been through with my horses, including the studies I'd made and the steps that I was taking to get them back to one hundred percent health.

As the conversation progressed, Greg asked what I thought about hoof boots and using them to aid in the healing process. I told him that I thought there may be a time and a place for them, but from my experience, in general, they were too difficult to put on. And once they were on, they would come off at the most inconvenient times. The boots I'd tried over the years just didn't seem to be the proper fit for horses. They simply weren't snug enough, or they rubbed, fell off, or dug into the hoof. And once you finally got them on so that they'd stay put it was almost impossible to pry them off. They were just a spare tire to use until the farrier arrived to nail on a lost shoe.

For the most part, Greg agreed with me. We both felt that hoof boots had their fair share of problems. However, we agreed these problems could be overcome. Greg then showed me the most unusual looking hoof boot I'd ever seen. In spite of its appearance, he insisted that it was the most durable, dependable and comfortable hoof boot on the market at that time, and it could be used for riding, too. He urged me to get a pair for my ailing horse, assuring me that they'd make all the difference in the world with her rehabilitation and recovery.

It was time to think differently. So I got a pair. As soon as I got back home, I tried them out. I was able to put them on Dot's feet all by myself, but admittedly, putting them on involved a lot more time, effort and attention than I would have liked. Nevertheless, I was tickled pink because it was immediately apparent that the hoof boots made Dot more comfortable.

It was amazing! Her posture, demeanor, body language and mannerisms all improved by leaps and bounds. Shortly after I'd put the hoof boots on her aching feet, her head dropped, and she licked her lips. In fact, by the very next day, even the sound of the hook and loop closures on the boots made her lick in anticipation of the comfort she would soon receive. Immediately, she was walking with no noticeable signs of pain or discomfort. And then, before I knew it, within weeks, she was running around pain-free with what seemed like boundless energy. It was more than I could have hoped for.

Although I'd suspected that nailing metal shoes to the bottom of a horse's feet was restricting blood flow, impeding circulation and having adverse effects on them in terms of shock-absorption, now I could plainly see there was a viable alternative.

New Partnership

As word continued to spread about Dot's success and the remarkable improvement of her health, more and more of my friends and fellow riders were coming on board, joining the ever-expanding barefoot brigade of horse owners. It was incredible. Going the natural route was starting to gain some momentum. The complaints I'd encounter had to do with tender hooves and the fit of hoof boots, which included the difficulties of putting them on and taking them off. I also heard gripes about them falling off when the horses were traversing over certain tough terrains. It was enough to make me want to discuss the matter with Greg, my new good friend from Australia.

Little did I know at that time, Greg had a long working history in footwear—for people. Greg knew a lot about designing and manufacturing all kinds of footwear, especially in the area of industrial safety work boots. Greg was also the managing director of a company called Old Macs Hoof Boots.

As we talked, he shared with me some hunches he had about why there were so many difficulties with these hoof boots for horses. Before long, the two of us came up with some clever solutions to the problems about which riders had been complaining for years. Our solutions were so simple we laughed and wondered aloud why no one else in the industry had experimented with them before.

We decided to form a partnership. Greg and I went on to design our new ideas for a hoof boot and have them patented and manufactured. With the improvements we made to the boots, we created the most durable, dependable and completely comfortable hoof boots for horses on the planet. Success!

After all the pain I saw in my horses' eyes and the struggle I went through to find solutions and healing, after all the flack I got for bucking the system by going barefoot and choosing hoof boots over metal shoes, it was all worth it to create a product that supports the health of my horses and yours.

The very best part of the story is that Greg and I formed an even stronger relationship. He came from Australia to live with me at my ranch in British Columbia, Canada, and we were married on the 8th day of the 8th month in 2008. We continue to live, love, play, work and run Cavallo together. Talk about synchronicity and destiny and equine romance!

6

WILD HORSES RUN FASTER

My search for knowledge and understanding of the history of horses required the study of everything horsey—a detached inquisitive mind, free of opinion, and a heart open to all possibilities.

Horses are timeless and adaptable. The earliest known horses existed 55 million years ago. Their early evolution was mostly as a response to changes in climate, and therefore, their living environments. As recently as 10 million years ago, over a dozen horse species inhabited the Great Plains of North America.

At that time, horses came in many shapes, sizes and colors, some as small as a large dog, and most horse species had three toes. Over time, adapting to a predominantly prairie life, the hoof evolved to the one toe form we are familiar with today. Eventually, the species equus dominated and survived.

There is discrepancy about how long man has interacted with and domesticated the horse—it's anywhere from 6,000-12,000 years. Our involvement with them contributed to how they evolved. Horses were hunted for meat and thus grew bigger and faster to survive. As their stature increased, humans used them for work or riding, which in turn made them larger and stronger. Even a hundred years ago they were primarily used for transportation and communication (like the Pony Express).

Now horses are bred less for work and more for competition or pleasure riding. Since domestication, we have created over 200 breeds of horses. How they continue to evolve will be determined to some degree by how we breed them.

Even wild horses are somewhat dependent on humans nowadays. Farming and cattle ranching as well as government requirements have limited wild horses' access to land, food and water. In some areas, wild horses aren't surviving very well and can get trapped—literally and figuratively—during natural disasters such as fire, floods or drought. For example, in the U.S., the Bureau of Land Management trucks in water for wild horses suffering during a drought. And (because horses arouse empathy in humans) in an effort to control the wild horse population, avoid excessive deaths on confined land and avoid the inevitably bad publicity that would come with it, the government is sterilizing and adopting out many wild horses. It is speculated that there are currently 30,000-40,000 wild horses in North America.

In Australia, there are over 1.2 million wild horses, called brumbies, in the Outback. With these numbers, the Australian government has been forced to cull the herds, flying over in helicopters and shooting them. It seems sad and certainly is controversial, but they see it as a nasty-yet-necessary measure. Between the 1.2 million brumbies and an additional 2 million wild camels wandering the Australian outback, food and water sources have become scarce—the impact extends to all natural wildlife.

A flood in Australia killed many domestic and wild horses a few years ago. While the ASPCA and other organizations were able to rescue some domestic horses, thousands of wild horses died as they were left to fend for themselves. The flood was so drastic that a rancher felt he had to shoot his 40 horses and 100 head of cattle. The animals hadn't eaten for over a week, and the water kept rising. He felt so guilty that, unfortunately, he then took his own life.

Similarly, not too long ago a huge fire swept across the mid U.S. and threatened the wild horse population. They were surrounded by fire and had nowhere to go. The horses had no help and no means to report their location. Too many were lost.

As we become more involved in the natural ecosystem and add to global warming, natural disasters are increasing in frequency. Fire, flood, and drought are more of a threat to horses than their mountain lion predators.

Horses, in their natural state, depend on their environment and are vulnerable, particularly to natural disasters. Their survival mechanism is their ability to instantly flee—to run as far and as fast as possible. This capacity necessitates healthy, strong hooves. Remember, these wild horses do not wear shoes. They are part of nature and are healthiest when treated holistically. They belong like the ebb and flow of the tides, the wind in the wild grasslands and the silence of a mid-winter night.

7

DANCING TO THE RHYTHM

Look around you. Patterns are everywhere. If you were to describe your surroundings what would you say? Do you see a garden made up of various flowers, each type of flower with a distinct pattern of petals and leaves? Do you see a trail of ants dutifully following back and forth from food source to the colony? Do you see a field temporarily turned into a parking lot for a local fair—no lines on the ground to follow, yet all the cars are parked in an organized fashion?

Now close your eyes and listen. Buh dum...buh dum...buh dum. Can you hear and feel your heart beat? Can you hear the rhythm of traffic or the beat of the rain on the window, the drumming of your horse galloping, or the consistent tempo of the birds chirping? The patterns and rhythms of our universe underscore our very existence and how we operate in this world. Being able to recognize and work with them makes life easier and more fun. Let me share with you what this can mean for you and your horse.

Universe of Patterns

Our universe is designed in patterns. Some are obvious and others less so. From the very structure of our cells to the consistent forms they make— human, horse, plant—it is all about patterns. Patterns don't just show up in how something looks or is built, but also in how it behaves. Behavior can mean actions, communication, and certain movements. Habits, good and bad, are patterns of behavior. The waves of the ocean or of sound, the alignment and rotations of the planets and moons, the barking of dogs, pecking of hens, and beat of music, all are patterns. Simply put, patterns are similarities, differences and connections that have meaning across space and/or time. If you can learn to recognize patterns, you can be in flow with them versus fighting them, or you can learn to influence them. As we strive to be in tune with our own wellbeing and to know and understand ourselves and our horses better, we have to take a step back and remember how we're part of a greater whole, our environment, all of nature, and the universe.

One pattern that consistently appears in nature, math, architecture, and art is a list of numbers called the Fibonacci Sequence. The man for whom this numerical sequence is named is Leonardo Pisano from Pisa, Italy. He called himself Fibonacci as in Filius Bonacci or "son of Bonacci" after his father. In the 13th century, Fibonacci studied arithmetic and found he most liked a Hindu-Arabic system that used ten digits and a decimal point. He is credited with being one of the first to introduce this system to broad use in Europe, which is what we use today. Part of Fibonacci's explanation of this system of mathematics included a particular integer sequence that starts with 0, 1, 1, 2, 3, 5, 8, 13, 21, 34, 55, 89, 144, 233....and so on. Each number in the sequence is the sum of the previous two numbers.

The significance of the Fibonacci Sequence is that it has been proven inherent to so many elements of nature. This pattern is demonstrated in biological settings, such as branching in trees, arrangement of leaves on a stem, fruitlets of a pineapple, flowering of artichokes, and the bracts of a pine cone, just to name a few. Many connect the sequence to the consistent pattern of nautilus shells and the curve of a wave and even breeding of some animals.

Related to the Fibonacci Sequence is the Golden Ratio, which is the ratio of the sum of two smaller quantities to the larger quantity is equal to the ratio of the larger quantity to the smaller one. The Golden Ratio shows in the arrangement of branches along the stems of plants and of veins in leaves, even in skeletons of animals and the branching of their veins and nerves. Scientists have also seen this pattern in the proportions of chemical compounds and the geometry of crystals.

Many artists and architects have used the Golden Ratio in what they call the Golden Rectangle as a template, believing this proportion to be aesthetically pleasing for what we find useful and beautiful in our modern world. An example is the Parthenon on Acropolis in Athens, Greece. The ratio is also used to calculate and demonstrate the rate and dimensions of growth for what is called the Golden Spiral. Its shape is tied closely to the Golden Rectangle. The Fibonacci Sequence combined with the golden ratio have also been popularized in culture as they are mentioned in novels like The Da Vinci Code, films, television shows, and songs.

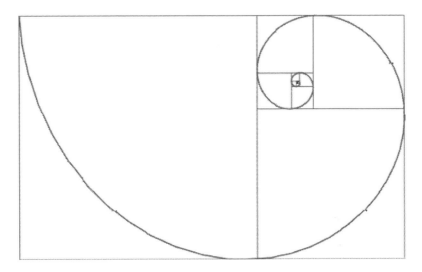

The Golden Spiral Overlaid by The Golden Rectangle

Patterns also universally show up as a result of the simple rules we innately or culturally follow. If every person or every member of a group follows the same short list of simple rules, then the group behaves in a coherent way as a whole. Have you seen a flock of birds take off from the brush? They may have initially taken to flight scattered, but they quickly come together, form a pattern and maneuver the wind as a unit and in the most aerodynamic way. They even maintain a consistent methodology if approached by a predator or if they come upon an obstacle. How do they know how to do that?

Horses do the same thing. If a stallion alerts the herd to danger, the lead mare takes off, dictating the direction and pace at which they flee to safety. The horses group closely together, often head over rump. You would think they would hurt one another running so quickly and tightly, but it keeps them safe. The birds and horses innately have a set of simple rules that they follow to know how to move.

As outsiders, we can see the pattern that these simple rules form. If you can see patterns in your horse's behavior and uncover the reasons or simple rules behind those patterns, you can understand him and work better with him.

Seeing and understanding patterns—be they in math or nature—can help you understand things and behaviors. Recognize these patterns for their familiarity and depend on the pattern to help predict the future.

Math and number patterns are all about prediction. Whether it is predicting what the 63rd number will be in a sequence, or how many pans of brownies you need to bake for the school, or how much feed you will need each month if you add three horses to the barn, recognizing number and behavioral patterns helps us solve problems. Patterns help us expect probability. Examples of probability waves include the rise and fall of populations of animal species as prey and predators wax and wane, the cycles of economic prosperity as resources and market confidences fluctuate, and the occurrence of diseases as biological defenses are activated in response to variations in genetic mutations and interventions.

Living Within Patterns

Sometimes we can let the probabilities hold us back from possibilities. If we come to depend solely on patterns, we don't have a chance to see what could change. I'm so glad I didn't fall into that trap.

When I first announced that I was moving to the country and buying a horse, my family responded with their assessment of probability for taking such action.

"Horses are worse than boats. You sink money in and get nothing back. They eat while you sleep. You can't afford it," my father told me.

I could have bought into it and accepted my status quo life, but my heart was pulling in an incontestable way—pulling me to horses. While the probability was that horses could cause me financial hardship and difficulty, all I could see were the possibilities of joy and love. So I went for it!

What I did not know was that I would encounter a mission. The practice of nailing metal shoes to horses' hooves would become so distasteful to me that I would devote my life to creating a better way. Patterns may be able to predict probabilities, but they can't necessarily identify and direct possibilities, at least not where the heart, imagination, and innovation are involved.

Rhythm of the Ride

Patterns of repeated sounds and silences create rhythm. A rhythm has a steady beat. Since you have surely listened to music if not also played an instrument or sang, you're very familiar with the nature of rhythm—long and short beats, fast and slow tempos. A single piece of music can incorporate many different rhythms. Rhythm isn't manmade, like some other patterns we've discussed, it's born out of nature.

There is rhythm in falling raindrops, the waves of the tide rolling in, the bark of a dog, the beat of your heart, the pulse in your veins, and the gallop of your horse. The patterns are a movement, be that the movement of sound or things, or both. Rhythm is flowing movement.

When I was first learning to ride, I noticed the rhythm of my horse. When I was able to connect to his rhythm, the ride was easier. If you connect to your horse's cadence when you're riding, you give your horse a lot more freedom of movement and create fluidity. If you can't, or choose not to realize that rhythm, then you force your horse to adhere to your own movement by adding force with bits, legs, strength, and muscle. I urge you to try not to control your horse. Give him some freedom. If you can surrender to the natural rhythms of the horse and his nature, riding him is like dancing with your partner. To get into the flow of that dance, I find it beneficial to listen to music while riding.

A great example of connecting to the rhythm of your horse can be seen in the discipline called Dressage Kur. Dressage Kur is a more formal English style of riding where the rider moves together with their horse in a dance movement to music. It is stunningly beautiful.

Dressage isn't the only discipline to feature this rhythm. I'll never forget the time I was at a reining competition called Super Slide. It was several years ago, and I had a booth at the event to promote my therapeutic saddle pads. The rides included fast spins, sliding, maneuvering horses in different patterns and showing off their abilities. While it is a more

Western style, it is based in dressage: control and movement together in a certain rhythm that is trained.

At the end of the night, three dressage riders wanted to show the western riders what they do. One of the dressage riders stopped by my booth before her ride. I told her all about my saddle pad designs. She shared with me that her horse seemed really stiff in the shoulders. She was frustrated because he was supposed to be a fluid mover and had been a big investment that she had flown over from the Netherlands. I gave her a saddle pad to try, and to my surprise she tried it in competition right then.

Most people don't put on a new piece of equipment in com- petition, but she did.

When the rider put on the saddle pad, her horse found that he had freedom of movement in the scapula. He was a big Dutch Warmblood, bred to perform and move. Saddled up and ready to go, just as this rider started her dance, her horse moved out, realizing he felt freedom of movement for the first time since he had been with her under the saddle she was using. He immediately remembered what he used to do. The rider wasn't ready for it, and she fell off! Even though I didn't see it happen, she came back to me at the booth afterward with her saddle pad in hand and with a stern look said, "I fell off my horse." I felt terrible.

Thankfully, she then giggled and went on to say, "All of a sudden I realized that my horse was moving properly the way he was meant to move for the breeding and money I paid to import him. Now I know he can really move, and I got what I paid for—but I had to fall off."

That's the difference that a freely moving horse can make! The scope of movement is limited for a horse that is hitched in cadence or if you're not in balance with him. If you're moving with him, and he is free, you can have a lovely dance. But sometimes we have to learn the hard way.

Recognizing patterns and therefore rhythm not only helps us understand and predict many things in nature and our lives, but it also allows us to influence them. A beaver influences the pattern of a river when he builds a dam. You may influence the pattern of your children not eating vegetables by having them help plant a garden the next year; being a part of how that veggie ends up on their plate can make them more interested in eating it. You can influence the patterns of your horse's rhythm as well. I certainly believe you make the best connection and have the best ride if you allow your horse's natural rhythm and get in sync with him. If you know his natural cadence—that his front left leg is going to pick up next, etc.—then you can orchestrate your cues to him to facilitate that movement as opposed to being contradictory to it. It's about timing.

Your horse will follow your direction because he is attentive and wants to please, but he also is listening to his own rhythm. Horses move in harmony with one muscle activating a joint and a bone and moving the body in cadence. You can see it, hear it and feel it as he moves. Beautiful!

You can influence which rhythm your horse is following through the cues you give him to move at different gaits. Each gait has its own rhythm, similar to different types of music. Your horse is an exquisite instrument— maybe even the entire orchestra. You can direct him while still respecting his nature and working with his natural rhythms.

8

CAN'T FOOL ME

There are several vibratory frequencies in the universe, some we can hear or feel and many we can't—or at least humans can't. Horses communicate in vibration frequencies with one another through subtle sounds and movements, many of which we can witness and some that we cannot. Certainly, they whinny and snort to express and communicate.

Rhythm is a key element of distinguishing and understanding meaning in human linguistics, just as there are patterns in the way your horse communicates with you, be it in his body language or his movements. We learn the sounds of our horses and their meanings similarly to how we recognize our own baby's cries and coos before they can speak.

There is a theory about non-verbal, non-visible communication, which is called limbic resonance. It is the capacity for sharing deep emotional states that arise from the limbic system of the brain engaging the dopamine and norepinephrine hormonal and emotional circuits. Drs. Thomas Lewis, M.D., Fari Amini, M.D. and Richard Lannon, M.D. first brought forward this idea in their book, *A General Theory of Love* (Vintage, 2001). They describe limbic resonance as the capacity for empathy and non-verbal connection and suggest that our nervous systems are not self-contained, but rather significantly tuned into those around us with whom we share a close connection.

They have found this to be true for all mammals and explain it as "a symphony of mutual exchange and internal adaptation whereby two mammals become attuned to each other's inner states." It is that unspoken knowing you have with your closest loved ones and with your horse. It is also that human condition of being able to sense empathetically pain or love in a stranger. You know how some people just make you feel great, and you come away from others wanting to go visit your therapist and get a happy pill? It stems from a resonance, a rhythm we cannot consciously sense but can feel subconsciously. It is part of the interconnectedness of all of nature.

Grounding

Imagine your pasture covered with the glistening luminosity of the morning dew as your horse meanders through his grassy environment, his bare hooves making direct connection to the earth. That's right— "connection"—and also conductivity, especially with wet grass. We call this "grounding." The transmission of electrical impulses from the earth is running freely up through his feet. Blood and body fluids are made up of these charged ions dissolved in water to comprise many fundamental functions in his body. The charged electrons run electrical energy throughout all the cells in his body. Humans have about 30 trillion of these cells; imagine the number of these cells in a horse's body, so much larger than your own.

Generating these electrical fields is essential to the transfer of free electrons from the ground into the body and throughout the tissues, keeping his body at the same negatively charged electrical potential as the Earth.

Allowing your horse to be barefoot facilitates this direct, *natural* connection. So that's part of the science, and there's a "feel good" factor as well. Try it yourself. Walking barefoot out in the morning dew can make you feel alive, invigorated, full of life force energy and as healthy and vibrant as your barefoot horse.

The 21st-century barefoot movement is leading the way back to what nature intended. Try leaving your horse barefoot when on his usual living environment and then use horse hoof boots to protect his soles on terrain other than which those hoofs are accustomed to and/or when he has the additional weight of rider and tack. It's a perfect alternative to nailing metal into their feet. If you want to make sure you get the correct hoof boot for your horse, please contact Cavallo. Our mission is to help.

Horses: Grounded and Connected

Horses, as prey animals, are delicately in tune with their environments. They are so connected to the earth and all of nature around them that they can hear and sense something far away. It is a planetary resonance, if you will. A slight crinkle of the leaves may alert them to a predator; their ear will twitch, and they'll launch into a run for safety.

Horses and other animals are literally grounded, sensing vibration patterns that we humans don't notice until the patterns are stronger. For example, in several instances of tsunamis, people have said they were warned by the animals' movements. Before the people became aware of the coming waves, the animals were seeking higher ground. If we can understand and be aware of the bigger universal sound frequencies, patterns, and rhythms, we could become more sympathetic that this is where our horse resides in the universal flow.

Journey with Wildebeests – Contrasting Equus to Antelope Deep in the Heart of Africa

Fast, full-size and four legged, the wildebeests of Africa have adapted to the danger of predators to behave just as our horses do. The language of equus warns to run when there's danger, stay together in a herd for safety, and that at least one must remain alert to warn others. It's the graciousness of perception, intuition and automatic response that keeps them alive.

Bumping through the vast expanse of the Kenyan Savannah, dotted with tens of thousands of various antelope, lived up to the #1 ranking of my bucket list. The Mara North Conservancy's 28,500 hectares is home to an assortment of plants, reptiles, birds, and among other wild animals, the striking zebra. I must admit, this species of equus held my interest. I even fantasized little Maasai children out there in the night braiding those perfectly patterned tails. Observing the delicate balance and functional patterns of hierarchy, I saw that zebra life is quite similar to any domestic horse herd.

Astonished to silence, we watched from the safety of our jeep as the remarkable wildebeest attempted migration, crossing the Mara River to head for the Serengeti. Problem is, there are crocs in those waters—big ones. The herbivores circled to a crossing, sensed the carnivorous danger lurking beneath murky waters and recoiled—en mass—running for their lives. They'd try again later, or in another spot. In its raw starkness the food chain is exposed by this, the biggest wild animal migration in the world. Imagine a massive rhino, lithe lions, camouflaged leopards, cheetah, buffalo, vultures, hyenas, jackals and warthogs all co-existing in seeming harmony until somebody gets hungry. Gazing on, I concluded that I am happy to remain with homo sapiens, comfortably ensconced at the top of the chain.

Everything is peaceful while the predators are satiated and then when hunger grumbles, the intuitive prey becomes agitated and nervous. I thought of the way we interact with our horses, at times quite mindlessly. We may approach with a steadfast inflexible agenda. We want something from them and we're thinking about that and not about them. Remember how intuitive they are and even that perceived pressure can make them edgy. Why not just hang out one day, watch and listen?

I never expected that just to hang out watching the age-old ebb and flow of nature would provide even more profound insight into our own beloved horses back at home. Even our tamed equine pals peacefully grazing in the field will revert easily to their innate survival skills when predators want something. Safari in Kenya will remain in my heart always as one of life's extraordinary "Ah Ha" experiences.

These animals are profoundly aware of present time. They are not ruminating about their brother who became breakfast for a lion last month or projecting their thoughts into the future by wondering if they, too, might become a snack, for whom or when. What would be the point of that? If they do not remain consciously aware, they might fail to notice the crouching cheetah racing directly at them. And we, too, have the power of *present moment* awareness. In fact, it is a conscious decision we can all make that can make the entire difference to our level of contentment. We cannot change the past or predict the future, so why waste our energy trying when instead, we can just be? How can we do that? There's one way that I know of: meditation.

9

THE FORGOTTEN ART OF STILLNESS

The present moment, if you think about it, is the only time there is. No matter what time it is, it is always now."

- Marianne Williamson

Meditation is not easy. It takes a lot of silence and stillness, which often make us feel uncomfortable. While you'll never have the innate connection to the earth that your horse does (because you're simply wired differently as a separate species), you are still part of nature and can increase your connectivity to the patterns of the world.

Meditation is the best way. Meditation requires that you stop focusing on the external and instead turn your attention inwards. It truly amazes me how few people are comfortable just sitting quietly alone. Always looking for distraction, it is difficult to be truly present with yourself and your horse.

A simple way to start is to focus on your breathing: find your own rhythm, feel the rise and fall of your diaphragm, become aware of your heartbeat. The most difficult and beneficial part of meditation, at least for me, has been observing my mind. I always go off on tangents and think about the strangest things—one little thing leading into another and all relatively meaningless. The challenge is to realize this distraction is happening and make an effort to come back to stillness.

For example, I went to my meditation cushion last night, sat down, took some slow deep breaths, closed my eyes and attempted to begin. I immediately interrupted myself: "Oh gosh, I should have called my son. Speaking of calling, why didn't Julie call me back? She's probably mad at me because I was so involved talking to Simone at the party. Her hair looked strange. That dangling curl. My hair is just like my mother's. Rodney's mother passed away. I must remember my mother's doctor's appointment. Oh, I have that meeting tomorrow. I should prepare. What will I wear? I really need some blue shoes to go with that skirt. It was really too expensive. Oh wait, where did I put my wallet?" And on it goes.

If it's really important, you can stop and write it down, but I assure you it's usually not worth it. It takes time, but as you practice and master meditation or any other method of silent connectedness, that internal focus actually allows you to become more in flow with the rhythms of nature, of the universe. You start to realize that you are not separate from the rhythms; your existences are interwoven.

If we go to a silent place and become more connected with our environment, we can exist in the same place as our horse, the same state of being. If your mind is busy thinking about dinner or what you're going to wear, you will be disconnected from yourself and your horse. We have more than 60,000 thoughts a day. That's quite a distraction in the future and the past. Yet our horse resides in the present. You will benefit if you meet him there.

Practice spending time in silence. Even if just for an afternoon, it's amazing how your experience of the world heightens. You hear things you wouldn't normally. You see things with greater depth of perception. It's much easier to access your intuition. And in this way you cultivate a clearer understanding of equus.

It is often only in stillness that we can sense a rhythm. You don't normally notice the rhythm of your breathing or the beat of your heart. Sometimes you must stand still to feel the rhythm of a machine or music in the distance. Regardless of how you find it, once you do you can lose yourself in it. It is like dancing when no one is watching. It is that synchronicity that creates a natural freedom. This is where the joy lies.

And if you think it's something flaky for those who live in a fairy tale, we don't have to go far to find other real people who have made a practice of silence or meditation a part of their lives, such as football player Joe

Namath, media mogul Rupert Murdoch, David Letterman, Clint Eastwood, Jennifer Aniston and Sheryl Crow, to name just a few.

Meditation helps release the past and disconnect from the future in order to truly be in the present moment. It allows the silence to listen to your inner wisdom and guidance from Spirit, God, and the Universe. Meditation keeps us grounded and focused.

Getting Started

When you're first learning to meditate it can be frustrating and very difficult to quiet the incessant chatter in your head. It may be easiest to start with guided meditations that help you steer your mind. You could also use a mantra, a word or phrase that you silently repeat as part of your breathing pattern. Some find that playing soft instrumental music in the background can be helpful as well. For me it's a distraction because I am always listening to find the melody. We're all a little different. It is usually not something you can jump into for long stretches. If you've never done it, try to be still for just two minutes. Just observe what it is you are thinking about. If you can quiet the mind to the point where you can track and be aware of your thoughts, the next step is observing the gap between the thoughts where your often overactive mind takes a break.

Once you feel you have mastered that, add a minute. There are people who have ritualized meditation in their lives for decades and only meditate for 15 minutes at a time. It is a skill that takes time to build but has tremendous proven benefits for your mind, body and spirit.

People say they don't have time to sit still. They are busy and what they do is very important. They are always running out of time. I get that, but let me tell you, if that is your perception, you will create it and soon you will indeed run out of time.

Learn to pause so good things can catch up to you. In fact, in many ways, taking some time makes you more productive and focused so that you actually can achieve more. Oprah Winfrey has been practicing meditation every day since she invited meditation teachers to Harpo Studios in 2011 to lead the entire company together in meditation at the beginning and end of the workday.

Oprah said, "That way of being 'still' with ourselves—coming back to the center and recognizing that something is more important than you—it's more important than the work you are doing, brings a kind of energy, an intention that we have never had before,"

The results were incredible. Her co-workers no longer had migraines, slept better and developed happier relationships with their friends and family, says Oprah, who recently partnered with Deepak Chopra to create a 21-Day Meditation Experience, which is a fun and easy introduction to meditation.

Connecting Through Breath

Deep breathing is another one of the simplest and most powerful ways to connect to the present moment. It is something you can easily do to stop whatever is rushing through your mind or body and instantly be present. Breathing deeply helps you get centered, focused and reduces stress. Physically, you are filling your system with fresh oxygen and flushing out toxins, both of which help you function better at the cellular level and beyond. What I also love about deep breathing is that you can do it anywhere, anytime and for any amount of time.

Try this: 1) be still, 2) close your eyes (unless you're driving), 3) take a deep breath in as you count to five, 4) hold it for a count of seven, 5) release it for a count of seven. Repeat this several times, each time taking in and releasing more air than you thought you could. And remember to release as much as you take in. When we're constricted, we hold our breath or even forget to breathe. It's hard to let your mind run off in its infinite unrelated ways when you are focused on the simple task of deep breathing. For all the stale air you breathe out, breathe in the new oxygen to nourish your cells.

Connecting at a deeper level to your rhythmic breathing can take you to the next level in performance, too. Finding the rhythm pushes you and allows you to do more than you think you are able to do, sometimes without even being aware of it.

Have you ever been at the gym on the treadmill or on a bike and you're working out at a normal pace, then you pop in your ear buds, turn on a high-octane playlist, and next thing you know you're running faster or longer than you thought you could? Your body got in sync with a rhythm that took you to that next level.

I've also witnessed it each year at the hunt here in my neighborhood. It's quite a traditional foxhunt, with dogs chasing the scent of a fox and the horses and riders following suit across the varied landscape. The excitement of the pack of dogs alongside the horses and riders is tremendously stimulating. There are three levels of trails for the hunt, including three levels of jumps. You can ride around the jump, take a small log, or glide over a substantially higher jump. Riders choose their path based on self-determined ability. Consistently, horses and their riders get caught up in the emotion and tempo of the ride and end up taking a higher level trail and jump than they intended. Both individually and in concert with their horse they are swept into pushing their performance to the next level.

The next time you ride, pay special attention to the beat, and you will resonate with the natural cadence of your horse. The rhythm will catch you, creating a deeper connection and allowing a freedom of movement that takes your experience and your horses' to a new level. Riding a freely moving horse is but one of the countless beautiful ways you can enjoy what so many only dream of. Life with horses is so much better when your horse is comfortable. So let's start connecting from the ground up.

10

WHOLE HORSE, WHOLE HUMAN

Horses are natural foragers. They like having to search for their food. In the wild, they eat shrubs, twigs, dry grass, and weeds. They are dependent on what they can find and have survived for millions of years this way. Horses don't need big grassy fields. They're actually meant to eat very rough substances. Rich grass ongoing can compromise their digestive systems. This is one of the reasons they survive well in arid areas.

The habitat and availability of food for wild horses is being compromised by the development and urban sprawl of humanity. In many ways, their future is in our hands. For their survival, it is important that we have a good understanding of their nature and their physical requirements.

It is the same as our health. The further we get from eating whole foods and a clean diet from nature, and the more we eat a diet excessive in processed food, we gain weight, get sick, and develop conditions we would otherwise not have—like diabetes. We live longer because of science, but I wonder at times if this is a good thing. Being kept alive artificially is fine as long as a reasonable quality of life remains.

I ponder this quite a bit now that my parents are in their 80s, and they are still healthy and vibrant—perhaps because when they were young things really were more natural for them.

Just as with us, there is an entire industry of products and services for horses to treat the conditions caused or exacerbated by not living holistically. These actions counteract nature's survival of the fittest and keep the weak alive. Sure, horses can get injured and become ill when they're out in the wild, but it can be compounded when they're forced together, too often kept confined and fed foods unnatural to them. Getting back to a more natural, holistic way of living is better for both us and for our horses. Let's treat the cause, not the symptoms. The liberal use of symptom treatment has given things like antibiotics panacea status, and now we're developing immunity to them. Quick fix cover-ups just don't work.

We introduce herds and horses to new diseases by traveling with them around the world. It isn't much different from how we can get ill when we travel and are exposed to things that people native to that land tolerate naturally. When we are in close proximity to someone who is sick, we have a greater chance of catching a virus. People often get sick after sharing the air on an intercontinental flight. Certainly, when a child gets head lice, soon enough the entire class has it.

Some of the products that are being offered in the horse community now are really not what a horse would eat in a natural environment. For example, the industry is starting to make feed based on beans or coconuts, which are not a natural food for them. If given a choice a horse would not choose beans. How would a wild horse crack a coconut shell?

Some businesses are trying to design feed that isn't always appropriate for horses. Others use sub-quality ingredients. Rather than discarding waste products like beet pulp and cornhusks, they package them up as desirable ingredients. How is that good?

Another example is the promotion of pure alfalfa as standard feed for horses. Alfalfa is really a better crop for cattle; it is used to grow them big quickly. Yet, we are attracted by its richness, and we like how it looks and smells. Then the marketing wizards sell it to us as "sun-cured" to pique our health consciousness. Here's the thing, there is no other way to cure alfalfa! We're being sold to as if we're getting something that is better than it is or that we're making a choice. It reminds me of when I see "organic wild salmon" on a restaurant menu; if it's caught wild, what else would it be? Recently I saw a bright orange starburst celebrating "gluten-free" on a bag of potato chips. So now this makes chips good for us? Right!

If we are what we eat, then we should use common sense. Whole, clean, organic foods are best. Note how our health shifted with the introduction of fast foods and mass-produced processed foods. Beware of genetically modified fruits, veggies, and grains. They have been altered for the benefit of the food industry, not ours, and they deplete the immune system. Isn't all of this true for both humans and horses? Yes. Be wary of trendy promotions; there is usually a downside. A people example of this is the plethora of fat-free and sugar-free products. Sounds great, doesn't it? Ah, but check the label; more often than not, in order to make the fat-free items taste OK there is an increase in the sugars and vice versa for sugar-free products. Also, look for pesticides. Some ingredients are more likely to have been grown with a high percentage of pesticides.

Horses need nutrients, but they survive well as foragers on seemingly simple roughage, too. In the spring, they get rich, juicy grasses and succulent new growth, which then changes with the season. In nature they will rummage until their body gets what it needs, roaming for 20 miles in a day if need be.

Depending on environment, hay quality, stress or activity level, you may need to support your horse's nutrition needs with supplements. The same rules apply—read the label and be diligent about quality. A lot of feed contains fillers and binders. Some contain glue to hold the pellets together. And it's not just feed. What about those supplements? The vitamin and mineral content in some compounds is so small it's bogus to think they could actually help your horse. Even if there is enough vitamin and mineral content, it's often not chelated and may not be readily absorbed in the horse's system. But the tack store shelves are laden with them. The bottom line here is you get what you pay for.

Digestion, Worms & Supplements

I'm not trying to tell you precisely what to eat or to feed your horse. I know you only want what is best. The food market is a big industry. I'm reminding you—and me—that it is easy to get caught up in pretty packaging and trends. This is true for both the food decisions we make for ourselves and those we make for our horses. The closer to what our bodies naturally need and crave, the better it is for our well-being, people and horses alike. I encourage you to question everything. Learn to read labels. Ingredients are listed in order of quantity. If sugar is first or second, there's a lot of sugar in the product. And if there are several things you can't even pronounce, put it down. Be a stickler for purity and quality. Navigate the care and feeding of your horse back to what he would experience in an appropriate wild environment, or at least close to it.

Just as you and I look for the highest quality nutrient-dense food for us and for our families, I believe it is best to do the same for our horses. After all, horses are part of the family. Be wary of the ingredients in feed the industry packages up and markets to us. Select feed and quantities of food based on the health and activity level of your horse. If your horse is more sedentary or older, he will need less food than if he is an extremely active competitor. An older horse may need his hay soaked to make it easier to chew and digest. Speaking of chewing, we need to take the teeth into account as well, and I will address that a little later in the section entitled "Long in the Tooth."

Take care in selecting supplements and pharmaceuticals. Quality is key. It is always best to try, or at least consider, natural remedies and preventative care over chemical compounds from big pharmaceutical companies. This line of thinking then opens the controversial issue of worming, which can be big business. I believe that many doctors over prescribe worming medication. Veterinarians used to take a more holistic approach and really visit with the horse. This kind of care has too often gone by the wayside, much the same as physicians have done in Western medicine for humans.

I do my best to take care of the basics first. Keep the paddock and stall clean and ensure they are free of manure. Make sure there is fresh air circulation. Outside, you usually want to have a bare minimum of an acre for every horse. If your horse is getting overrun with worms, too frequently it could be due to his nutrition, or you may need to get more diligent picking up manure. If he has a healthy immune system, he will be able to ward off an overabundance of worms and keep a healthy gut balance. It is the same with our health.

If we humans eat a lot of processed foods with little nutrition, it may start to affect our health and immune system function. That makes us more susceptible to catching a cold or other illness. For your horse, over-worming with drugs can deplete the immune system of natural defenses.

Some say that the best times to worm are early in the spring after the last frost and in the fall after the first frost. If you're concerned about worms or the health of your horse's digestive tract, have some feces examined so you can really know what you're dealing with.

Human and horse digestive systems are somewhat similar in what they need to stay healthy. We both need to keep a healthy balance of the right bacteria in our bowels. This is particularly important for parasite control in horses. We all need to minimize the sugars we take in. Even though a horse may not be consuming sugary sodas or desserts as we do, too many carrots or fruits with high sugar content can be just as bad for him. Before I learned all this, I fed one horse bananas because he loved them. Big mistake! While your body needs greens and fiber for health and wellness, so does your horse—and he gets his with grass, leaves, and twigs.

It is good practice to give your horse a cycle of probiotics after a worming to help rebalance the natural flora in the digestive tract. I have found that probiotics really should be kept refrigerated, even if the packaging doesn't direct you to do so.

Human bodies want to be in an alkaline state—that's around a pH of 7.4. Food choices and stress can make the body more acidic, which in turn leads to disease and acidosis. Bottom line: Do your best to fuel with quality nutrition and supplements, and keep the harsh synthetic drugs and fancy packaged food products to a minimum. Taking care of your horse's physical being is central to his overall well-being. Providing exercise, safety, shelter, quality nutrition, and hoof care are all ways to ensure a happy, healthy four-legged friend. Your horse's grace, beauty, and strength are diminished or emboldened by his physical health. I feel in my heart that caring for this glorious creature is an honor. We have a deep love and commitment to our horses and in some cases will even risk our lives for theirs. I joke with my friends that I have worked hard all my life for the privilege to spend regular joyous hours shoveling manure! The non-horsey ones don't get it.

Glory Be

My friend, Dr. Tomas Teskey, is a veterinarian and the author of *The Unfettered Foot* and *Breaking Tradition*. He wrote a beautiful story that demonstrates connecting with a horse on many levels. He gave me permission to include it here for you.

He calls the story "Glory Be."

∞

CAROLE HERDER

It was raining lightly this monsoon season in Arizona, and near dusk as I drove the 35 miles before pulling off the highway at a farm new to me—the call had come in just as I reached home, where all my own animals and young daughters awaited my return. The old man's weak, raspy voice relayed a short story, most of which I did not fully comprehend, save for some key words such as "horse"..."mud"..."down"..."slippery"... I was off again after fueling up on some quick hugs and kisses, back out to the truck with a container of soup and two pieces of bread.

Sudden, slick mud stimulated me to reach for the four-wheel drive as I worked my way up to the old wooden farmhouse. I left the truck running, the radio playing some country music song while the wipers and defroster tried to keep the windshield clear. I quickly trotted through the rain and around the puddles of rainwater along the driveway, and up the wooden stairs to the front door of the house, where I was soon greeted by an elderly man in overalls, face drawn, not speaking much but simply mumbling in a raspy voice I recognized—something about a horse as he pointed towards the barn further down the lane. "Just put her down, Doc... just put her down" were the last words I made out as I nodded in understanding and turned back to the truck, hunching my shoulders against the rain and biting wind.

I pulled down the lane and parked before a creaky old wooden gate and proceeded in my attempts to locate the "down" horse—not in the barn, not in the alley. Sloshing through the mud in a circle around the barn, I suddenly spied the rear end of a bay horse laying on its side. As I worked my way around to get a better look, a very pregnant mare appeared, with her front end half submerged in a pool of muddy water that had accumulated under the edge of the barn. The water was running off the roof in hundreds of tiny streams, continuing to fill the pool, when a sharp clap of thunder directly overhead opened up big holes in the low clouds, releasing heavy, cold drops of rain that now picked up the tempo, beating down more furiously on the tin roof. One nostril of the beast was under water and blowing bubbles, which impressed me—not something I had ever witnessed.

Without really thinking, I waded into the cold water behind the horse and lifted her head, one hand under her nose, the other grabbing her ear. She took several big breaths as her muzzle came clear of the pool. She seemed to be resting in my grip, but then suddenly became tense and agitated, attempting to get up. Her front end was downhill, and her cold body was stiff and uncooperative. As she lunged, I had no choice but to let her head go, and it splashed back down into the water. It was starting to rain harder now. All at once I realize there are no other farms for miles, there's an old man in the farmhouse that wants me to euthanize this horse, but the horse is going to drown first, and I am going to have to watch her die.

After watching her blow bubbles from her one submerged nostril once again, I turned and raced back to my truck, idling just outside the barnyard. Throwing open the rotten board gate, I proceeded to drive my truck through thick mud down the lane alongside the barn. Reaching the end, I did a half turn and began to back towards the rear corner where the mare lay in the pool, where the water was continuing to run off the roof and submerge her front end. Tearing open one of the trunks I had behind the vet box, I hurriedly selected the sixteen-foot cotton rope that I normally used to tie hind legs forward when gelding colts.

Wading out into the cold water again—which was now halfway to my knees—I searched beneath the muddy surface for a hind leg and tied a quick loop around her pastern, throwing the rest of the line back toward the truck. She began to struggle as I tightened the loop, and I fell backward into the pool, the icy water soaking every inch of me. Scrambling backward through the water away from her kicking legs, I righted myself and looked back at the mare. She had now slipped further into the deepening pool, her head completely submerged now, save for one ear pinned back and quivering.

I slogged back out to her, wet and cold and crying and cursing. One hand under her nose, one grabbing her ear, I squatted and lifted her tired head once more. Her third eyelid worked in concert with her other lids to clear the mud, and she heaved big breaths of humid summer air. I don't know how long I stood there holding her head...

—I can still hear the rain pecking away at that roof like a snare drum, full streams of cold water running off the roof and filling the pool.

—I can still smell her wet head in my lap as my soaked boots sink into the slimy mud beneath me.

—Time stood in surreal stillness. The drumming of the rain on the tin roof drowned out my frustrated cries for help.

—Just me, a horse, the mud, the rain and the pool of water—a perfectly orchestrated moment in time, crafted in an especially dismal setting.

I heaved cold air and just cried.

And I just began to talk to her softly as the rain fell, and the water level rose to my knees. Then I looked back at the idling truck, and the end of my rope at the edge of the pool.

In the same, resigned, soft tone of voice, I told her my plan. "I'm going to leave you again, girl, but I won't go far. I promise I will not leave you until this is over."

I allowed her time for another big breath and released my grip slowly, watching her head completely disappear under the water, bubbles welling up as she exhaled. I let her go.

Finding the end of my rope, and determining it was still secure around her hind pastern, I slid my way out of the pool and hurried back to the cab of the truck. I quickly drove in reverse to the edge of the pool, secured the emergency brake, flew around to the rear and tied the end of the rope around the ball hitch on the rear bumper. Glancing over my shoulder as I returned to the driver's seat, I noted that the surface of the water over her head was still, save for the ripples and dancing droplets everywhere as the rain continued to fall. The exposed side of her belly was above the surface, quivering in a way that told me she was dying.

I let-off-the-brake-engaged-drive-and-hit-the-gas
simultaneously. Just a couple of feet of slack and the truck came tight with the rope. What little angle I had between my hitch and the mare's hind leg suddenly straightened out, and I hit the gas one more time, all four wheels churning mud and manure. As I peered backward out the open window, mud from the left front tire covered my head as I worked the steering back and forth. It wasn't enough...it was just too slick, the horse too heavy and anchored downhill in the pool of water.

I reversed again to the edge of the pool, looked straight ahead, and with my teeth clenched, hit the gas as hard as it would go, all four wheels churning copious amounts of mud, trying to find purchase in the hopelessly slick barnyard soup. Suddenly, the front end caught purchase on something more solid underneath the goo, and the truck, rope, and horse lurched forward!

We were free of the water.

...And she lay still in the rain except for the quivering in her flanks as I returned to her, mud covering her eyes, nose and mouth, her pale and bluish tongue hanging lifeless and limp...it was too late. I kneeled at her head, wiping mud from her nostrils. There were tiny twitching muscles all over her face and neck and down through her body, like so many other animals I had witnessed dying before my eyes.

And then I wondered—what if? I positioned myself between her front and hind legs and came down on her chest with all the weight of my soaked behind—what could it hurt? She was dead. Watery bubbles spilled from her nostrils, and after a second and then a third pummeling from my butt on her chest, I thought I saw her ear twitch! Just a fluke—probably just movement from my jumping on her that caused her head to move—oh well—keep going. Once, twice, and one more time. And the mare gurgled and began to struggle! I'm sure I exclaimed something appropriate to indicate how flabbergasted I was that the horse was moving—and BREATHING! Now, I've never been accused of having anything even remotely resembling an ample backside, but at that moment I remembered thinking that was the most useful thing I'd ever done with it—performing CPR on a horse.

I got myself clear. By the time I had the rope free from her hind leg, she was shaking her head and bringing herself to a sternal position! Only seconds later, she jumped straight to her feet and trotted off down the lane, whinnying an intense and joyful song I remember to this day. I stood there in the mud, then fell to my knees, shaking uncontrollably from cold, wet skin and an adrenaline-soaked body. After straightening back up and standing on my own two feet, I attempted to check her over more carefully, but she was decidedly not interested in any further socializing with me at that time—I couldn't catch her as she ran circles around that barn! I watched her and her big pregnant belly make turn after turn around the barnyard and up and down the lane, avoiding the pool with a wary eye, stiff and cold, but with both ears forward and with surprisingly little lameness as the rain continued to fall. The percussion on the roof was still keeping the rhythm of the moment, and I noted with some anxiety how the streams of water now overflowed the pool where she lied unconscious moments ago.

I sloshed my way back to the truck and maneuvered back out the gate and up to the house, up the wooden steps, and knocked on the door. Soon, the elderly fellow appeared behind the screen door, checkbook in hand, red-eyed and his hands shaking, a tear running down his face. I stood there, dripping mud and looking like someone fresh from the county mud-wrestling tournament. I waited patiently until his eyes met mine, and I spoke.

"I couldn't very well check her out where she was laying in that water," I began to explain. "And when I pulled her out of the puddle with the truck, she jumped up and ran off! I'm sorry. Maybe I can come back by later and see if she will let me check her over a bit better?"

Looking puzzled, and then in sheer disbelief, his tears began to flow freely from his wide eyes as he stepped through the door onto the porch, peering through the rain toward the barn and catching a glimpse of the mare as she trotted up and down the lane. I stepped aside and didn't recount the real story to him, though I wonder now about whether he thought I was some sort of incompetent vet with how filthy I was. He pulled his cap down firmly over his eyes and stepped off the porch.

"What's her name?" I asked.

"Glory," he clearly replied without looking at me as he walked through the mud down the lane, calling to her, the rain continuing to fall.

Epilogue: Two months later, I drove by that same farm on a sunny day, and slowed long enough to peer down the lane past that old farmhouse, where Glory stood with ears erect, a bay foal at her side.

℀

I am grateful to Dr. Teskey for this story. It highlights the drama that can quickly unfold in a crisis. And the way to get through is to remember your purpose, follow your heart and keep calm. When you have some tools like deep breathing or a meditation practice, it can help prevent getting swallowed by the tragedies we all encounter from time to time. Your inner resources can support a detached level of observation as events unfold. The ability to somewhat remove yourself from the emotion of the drama will allow you to make better decisions in handling the actual event.

Understanding Your Horse

The more we can remember that our four-legged friends are the gentle power of nature personified, the better we can care for them in their domesticated state. Understanding and acknowledging the horse's history and how human involvement has played, and continues to play, a role in their evolution and survival is a reminder of the impact you have on all the horses with whom you come in contact. We bear a tremendous responsibility to give our best care and love to these creatures and respect their connectedness to their environment and natural living. This consideration extends even past our life with horses and points to our relationship with the natural world. Harmony and understanding are the keys to survival. Horses are our muses.

Changing Tides

Horses are herd animals and act accordingly. Other animals and humans can function like herds when we follow the tide of everyone else, when we accept the status quo. Think of lemmings that will follow one another off a cliff to their death. Have you ever been at an event when the crowd is moving much more slowly than you would expect? When you get to the front, you realize it is because everyone was trying to get through the same two doors without trying doors three through six. We also used to smoke on airplanes, not wear seat belts in cars, and not believe in interracial marriages. We didn't use to think a thing about nailing metal shoes on hooves and its dangers. We never questioned it. The tides can change, and they do. It requires that you first trust your true self. You also must be willing to differentiate between good and bad in everything. That takes your intuition, a gut check and a willingness to go off book from the standard way. Stop and recognize the beauty in the variation. Be conscious of what is around you. Trust your gut; pay attention to your intuition vs. being a lemming. Stop at the edge of the cliff and question why you're jumping.

There is always a tipping point when what were once the actions of a rebellious few become the accepted norms and institutional awareness of the new way of thought and action.

It is like the story of the Hundredth Monkey. Researchers studied a secluded island and its monkey inhabitants. One day the researchers left a sweet potato on the beach. A curious monkey picked up the sweet potato to eat. It was dirty and sandy, so he discarded it. Another day the monkey had an idea and washed the sweet potato in the ocean water. Eureka! The researchers began leaving more and more sweet potatoes to determine learning and transformation patterns with the monkeys. Each new monkey on the beach would go through a process of learning how to wash a sweet potato.

Soon the entire colony of monkeys was doing the same. The researchers went to a neighboring island with similar monkeys. They started the experiment again. This time, the monkey knew immediately to wash the sweet potato in the ocean. But how? There was no communication across the ocean. The one monkey's call for intuition led him to change the tide and ultimately the institutional knowledge and know-how of all monkeys.

What tide are you setting forth, what patterns are you creating by the thoughts, words, and actions you use with and around your horse? If you corral those thoughts and tend to them based on what your gut is telling you is true, you'll further connect with your horse and create the relationship you want.

Trust Your Gut

Just as we often look for the labels and accolades of and from others for guidance and approval, we tend to use the same method to give credence to our own value. We look for things like "four out of five doctors agree" or "rated #1." We lean on the labels of mother, driver of a certain type of car, president of the PTA, director of XYZ department. Your true self isn't a construction of labels. It isn't because of your resume that your horse will have trust in you or you in him. It is the core of your being, the true self that communicates with your horse. Your true self is most readily accessed through your own self-awareness and observation. If you want to be trustworthy, be honest. Your horse will thank you.

If you can connect to and trust yourself, you allow your true self to create your perspective, relationships, and interactions with the world. The true self is not ego-based, but holistic. You open yourself to more honest, loving, and trustworthy experiences when you drop the ego. If you enter the barn with this intention, shedding the ego, being your true self, you will have the best possible connection with your horse. You'll understand and trust him, and he will you. Any fear you may have will fall by the wayside.

Know that unless chemically imbalanced or extremely disturbed, your horse will never intend to harm you. If you enter his space with the intention of a true self-connection guided by intuition, your horse will meet you halfway. He doesn't care that you're a CEO who's preoccupied with your stressful day. He does know whether you are connected, and for him the energy he senses is real.

I have no idea what might pop out of the cauldron of all possibilities on any given day, either out of just pure spontaneity or as a result of previous actions. Either way, the only thing I have control over is my thought process and behavior. This is my choice.

"Take responsibility for the energy you bring into this space. "

- Jill Bolte Taylor, www.drjilltaylor.com

Dr. Jill Bolte Taylor is a neuroscientist who documented her own stroke. Through this amazing ordeal, she discovered that in many ways we are our own responsibility. How we show up is up to us, and we have a choice.

Mirror, Mirror In The Barn

One of the best truth-telling detectors is a simple mirror. How we feel, our mood, our pain or joy, years of laughing, hard work, pampering or laziness can be seen in a mirror. Horses can be mirrors of us, an indication of how we are showing up when with them. So if your horse gives you attitude, grumpiness or fear, first check yourself. Is he mirroring what he is sensing in you?

The Face of Pain

The French-born fashion designer, Coco Chanel, is one of the business women I respect most. She was listed in Time Magazine as one of the top one hundred most influential people of the 20th century. One of her fabulous quotes comes to mind when I have a good look at various faces. She said that at age 50 you get the face you deserve. I am seeing how women age in very different ways: wrinkles in certain areas, stress lines around a tense jaw or deep worry lines on the forehead. Have you ever noticed that some faces simply appear more pleasant than others? Some appear happy and relaxed while others look miserable or distressed. For us, it's about the way we've lived our lives.

As far as facial expression goes, it's somewhat the same with horses. Their pain, worry or anxiety appears in their face. Although unlike us humans who can carry the memory of stress and anxiety with us for years even after the cause is gone, horses are more able to lose the distressed appearance as soon as they lose the cause of it.

I have two quite different horses, whose faces show very different expressions. My barrel horse, the magnificent Dot, very quickly and more often can appear worried or anxious. Her eyelids get that peaked appearance, stiff in the center, tented over her eyes. I think she has a bit of a nervous stomach, perhaps from early performance stress, maybe even ulcers.

Her mouth becomes tense, and rather than having a relaxed jaw, her chin juts downward creating an angle, rather than flowing in line with her lower jaw. Her nostrils stress and flare out from center. Her ears can become stiff and pointed back, wider at the top than the base. Although over the years, these signs have receded, they still do appear from time to time and indicate a level of discomfort. It means I have to pay attention and go through the list of possibilities. Is it a stone bruise, perhaps an abscess, maybe too much fresh grass?

My other horse, the brave and fearless Slash (fearless, except around dogs, which is actually the reason for his name, Slash. I'll explain that later) only shows any of these signs occasionally, and it's usually a very obvious reason for pain. So with him the cause of his "long face" is more obvious.

When you look at your horse's face the next time, have a good look. Is there stress or relaxation? Pain or comfort? Your horse doesn't attach any labels, presumptions or stereotypes to you. He is relating to you as a being and reflecting what he is experiencing. If changing your attitude and emotion doesn't shift his, be sure to check his physical well-being. If he is despondent, agitated or grouchy, then look and listen for any discomfort he may be presenting.

Strip away your presumptions and expectations of self and others before you walk into his space. Be present with your horse. A horse can offer a reflection of your true self more honestly than any human being. You will see in your horse how you present in the world. If you are not being and living with integrity and honesty in your day-to-day life, and if the actions you are taking in life are not congruent with who you truly are, the disconnect will be evident in the interactions and relationship with your horse. Horses can smell it a mile away.

It is difficult to be present for yourself or whatever you are trying to achieve if you're preoccupied with something else. Have you ever driven somewhere and you suddenly are there but you are not sure how you got there? You don't remember the drive. You don't remember the other cars on the road, the traffic lights, the things you passed by, but here you have arrived and are getting out of the car. When you are preoccupied like this, you cannot be fully present.

Being around horses requires you to be present because you must be fully present and aware to both care for them and not be hurt by them. Being with horses is an opportunity to reflect.

Am I present?

Am I aware of everything in my surroundings?

Am I putting myself in danger?

Am I sure of the agenda of our time together?

Is this how I feel most in tune with my horse?

Is this how I want to feel?

Sometimes being present and honest with who you are and what you feel when you are with your horse can open you to new opportunities. Maybe you feel more of a connection when jumping logs in the bush rather than the barrel racing you've done for years. When you stop having expectations of how things should be and instead allow yourself to experience how they are and what they can be, you can reach a new level of honest relationship with yourself and your horse.

One of my favorite sayings is by the late Dr. Wayne Dyer: "When you change the way you look at things, the things you look at change." Be open to the four-legged mirror in front of you as a way to see into your heart.

The Courage to Think for Yourself

When I first got involved with horses, I didn't know much about them. I accepted the perspectives of those around me without question. It didn't take too long before I knew that "the way" was not my way and didn't align with my core beliefs. Have you been in a situation where you're wondering what you're doing there? You realize that you're practicing what everyone else is practicing and that's not really you? Be wary and question.

There is a big agenda in the horse industry on the whole as well as within different barns. You may be led to get involved with the dominant approach of a particular barn or trainer.

Like me, you may be encouraged to start doing what they're doing—get the same trailer and special equipment, pay various registration fees, use certain feed, etc. Unlike me, you may suddenly realize this isn't who you are or the vision you had before you got your first horse, yet you're all caught up in it.

I am no longer that cowgirl image I created with my partner, Rocky, but I am grateful for the experience and all the things I learned along the way. I am no longer the educated city girl either. Nor am I in any way bored or docile. The current version of me is truly the most authentic yet. If feels like the real me to be a truth seeker and even more to be so excited and passionate about the work I'm doing now to help horses. This is a whole new path that seems like the most obvious and natural next step.

For Pleasure or Pressure?

A part of our industry is based on that traditional "pressure" approach, as many barn owners and trainers earn their income by promoting a particular methodology. It supports a little cash machine. Some people really just want to trail ride but find themselves in the show ring.

I see this frequently with kids. They are stressed out with the most miserable expressions on their faces because of this tension and pressure to perform. All they get is "try harder" messages from their parents and trainers. This was supposed to be fun, yet the kids are not enjoying themselves. How can anyone be happy with that pressure? Being with your horse in today's day and age should be about joy and pleasure, not as much about work and transportation. If you're following a path laid out by your trainer or barn that isn't enjoyable, then pause long enough to determine if that is really how you want to work with your horse.

Friends, family, and local experts will always offer advice. In fact, I'm offering advice now. But I also am challenging you to think for yourself. Don't accept practices because they've always been done that way. Be willing to question practices and trust your intuition to know what is good for your horse and in line with your beliefs.

For me, that includes challenging the long-held belief that nailing metal shoes on our horse's feet is necessary. Don't get stuck in what others are telling you. Your responsibility is to take care of your horse, not follow every order from someone else. We have horses to bring pleasure to our lives, so how you work with them should be joyful. Joy has a frequency that resonates throughout your life, your family, and your very being. Your horse will feel it, too.

When I first got involved with horses, I got completely sucked into it. My previous husband suffered for it, too. He was threatened by my attention to horses. Unfortunately, our relationship was becoming increasingly difficult anyway. I think he was resentful about the time I was spending with the horses and would have wanted more control over this irresistible interest that flowed like a river into every crevice of my consciousness. There was no turning back and no point paddling against the flow. I was much younger then, and although I tried, I couldn't find a way to fix it.

However, being with my horses to care for them and learn about them gave me profound joy and fulfillment. I think it was wonderful for my kids as well, as they could see my level of commitment and responsibility. In a way, the household was a happier place because mom was fulfilled with life.

When you attain the joy you are seeking in keeping an animal, understand and live in harmony with that animal, it can resonate to so many facets of your life. I worked harder in my businesses; it added a level to my life that made everything more definitive and purposeful. You either are or are not a horse person. You have a life besides horses, and I know that. But the horse needs to be a big positive in your life.

Be open to all points of view, yet forge your own path in how you build a relationship with and care for your horse. Use the gifts of senses and intuition to communicate with your horse and guide you to what is best for him and congruent with your beliefs. You and I are similar in our approach or you wouldn't have been attracted to this book, so I want to support you in that. Horses are in our lives today more for joy and pleasure, not so much for work or transportation. It is important that you always interact with your horse with positive emotions, as he will be a mirror of your own vibrations and energy. Anything negative will impact the relationship and your horse. If you can just relax, you will both get more out of your time together.

I'm reminded of Pat Parelli's saying, "Smile with all four cheeks." I thought of that every time before going into the competition arena. I knew that if I entered the ring stressed out thinking, "Oh my God, I have to perform and really achieve something here; I have to place," my horse would not only sense the stress but physically feel it in how my body was connected to his. That stress transfer would impact our performance and suck the joy out of it.

It makes me sad when I see parents pushing their young riders to compete, and you can just see it on their little made-up faces that they aren't having fun, that they would rather be doing something else with their horse. No matter what you do with your horse, show or don't show, compete or don't compete, I encourage you to pause long enough to be honest. If it is great, carry on! If not, change it. Deepak Chopra says it's pretty simple. "It's either yum or yuck." Of course, we want yum. When you're with your horse it should be pure joy, anything else is a waste of time. I have a fun little chant while I gallop along the trails. I simply sing, "I ride for joy. I ride for joy!"

Predators We Are

Know this: Your horse is an honest being that will always show you exactly who he is and how he feels. Whether what you're seeing is emanating from him or is rather a reflection of you is something you'll have to figure out. Be aware that he is a prey animal and you are a predator. With this understanding, you can use techniques to negate your horse's innate wariness toward you and better convey your intentions of safety and love.

Take time to play and open your relationship with your horse to a deeper level of trust. Being honest with yourself and your horse and living congruently with your values will reflect in the interactions and joy you experience with your horse.

Sometimes when I need little reminders of how to be (be, *not do*), I post affirmations and meaningful quotes around my home and barn. It's often just enough to shift the energy.

Noticing Symptoms

You love horses. If you have one, you want the best for him. The fact that you are seeking more thoughts and further education is a testament to that, too. More than that, it's just part of being a horse person. We all love our horses and want them to be healthy and happy.

But maybe you're occasionally concerned that things aren't quite right with your horse. Does he sometimes seem a bit uncomfortable? Have you ever noticed issues like tripping when he goes downhill? Maybe he was OK last time, but for some reason now he won't pick up the correct lead, or today his ears are pinned, or his tail is swishing, or he seems just a bit agitated.

Maybe when you give him a little stall rest or some glucosamine product these symptoms abate, but then time goes on and others appear: lameness, stiffness, an odd smell coming from his feet, or just general unwillingness. I'm sure you can think of a time when you noticed rigidity, lethargy, heat in the legs and pasterns, or a time when your horse wouldn't pick up his feet for the farrier.

Most horse owners experience problems like these at some point. If not addressed, a horse's discomfort can result in bad behavior ranging all the way from biting, cribbing, weaving, rearing and to becoming quite dangerous.

We've all experienced various things—many people will tell you they're just part and parcel of owning a horse. I was an adult when I got my first horse, so I came from a blank slate. I had no clear idea of what horses should be, except for watching them running wild and unencumbered on the National Geographic channel. When I raised concerns about problems like these, you already know the story... "That's just how it is. Get used to it."

11

NATURE'S HONESTY

Horses don't contrive to deceive you. I have heard people say, "My horse is lazy. She's pretending to be lame because she doesn't want to go out for a ride today (or doesn't want to work)." That's ridiculous. Horses don't do that; they can't pretend or fake how they are feeling. It is natural, I suppose, to read more into your horse's behavior and her intentions because people often are not what they seem. However, that truly is not the case with horses. They aren't like people. They don't manipulate or play games. A horse limping is not faking an injury to get out of training the way a kid might put a thermometer to a light bulb to fake a fever and stay home from school. Horses don't scheme. Horses are innocent, honest, and of the highest integrity.

Having said that, we can teach our horses how to behave, but that's another matter. It's similar to a baby crying when he wakes up because he doesn't want to sleep alone. If you go to him, he learns that crying alleviates his loneliness and that you will come when he cries, and if you come every time he cries he may not learn to comfort himself. It's a complicated issue, and I only bring it to your attention to illustrate learned behavior.

Could it be that when we humans look for alternative meaning behind a horse's actions or mood it is because we don't want to accept that our horse may be displaying a level of discomfort or fear? If we acknowledge discomfort or fear from our horse, then we must take responsibility for resolving it and potentially owning that we may be the cause of it. That's a lot more difficult to admit and accept than saying our horse is trying to pull a fast one. It's an easy way out. If something's not right then it's not. Most people sense in their intuition or heart when something is wrong, but they may not want to look into it because they don't know how to resolve the potential issues. That leaves many horses living with a little discomfort that is being glossed over because their owners can't take action or don't know what action to take to deepen their knowledge.

CAROLE HERDER

It is easy to just follow the basics of what the industry says, i.e. "nailing metal into their feet protects their hooves." It takes courage and an open mind and heart to look for the answers and develop understanding beyond industry standards. The horse may be a complex animal physically, but emotionally he is simple and honest. He will show you how he feels if you can develop the savvy to see.

The following is my friend Joe Camp's story about how his life, focus, values, and perspective changed dramatically and quite unexpectedly.

ஒ

Blame it on Cash

By Joe Camp, best-selling author of The Soul of a Horse.

It was all Cash's fault.

This sudden loss of my sanity.

But how can you not love Cash?

The nicest, sweetest, brightest, most polite, gentlemanly horse I've ever met. The horse who not only taught us how to have meaningful relationships with horses but with people as well. The huge guy on four legs who taught us more about leadership, patience, and persistence than any two-legged ever had. The dear friend who quite simply changed my life when he said to me of his own free choice, I trust you.

I remember that it was an unusually chilly day for late May, because I recall the jacket I was wearing. Not so much the jacket, I suppose, as the collar. The hairs on the back of my neck were standing at full attention, and the collar was scratching at them. There was no one else around.

Just me and this eleven-hundred-pound creature I had only met once before. And today he was passing out no clues as to how he felt about that earlier meeting, or about me. His stare was without emotion. Empty. Scary to one who was taking his very first step into the world of horses.

The sales slip stated that he was an unregistered Arabian. And his name was Cash.

I was in that round pen because a few weeks earlier, my wife, Kathleen, had pushed me out of bed one morning and instructed me to get dressed and get in the car.

"Where are we going?" I asked several times.

"You'll see."

Being the paranoid, suspicious type, whenever my birthday gets close, the ears go up and twist in the wind.

She drove down the hill pulled into a park. There were a few picnic tables scattered about. And a big horse trailer.

The car jerked to a stop and Kathleen looked at me and smiled. "Happy birthday," she said.

"What?" I said. "What??"

"You said we should go for a trail ride sometime." She grinned. "Sometime is today."

Two weeks later we owned three horses.

We should've named them Impulsive, Compulsive, and Obsessive.

I had vowed that Monty Roberts' Join Up would be our path. Because the horse is allowed to make his own decision. It is his choice whether or not to say I trust you. We would begin our relationship with every horse in this manner. Our way to true horsemanship, which, as I would come to understand, was not about how well you ride, or how many trophies you win, or how fast your horse runs, or how high he or she jumps.

I squared my shoulders, stood tall, looked this almost sixteen hands of horse straight in the eye, appearing as much like a predator as I could muster, and tossed one end of a soft long-line into the air behind him, and off he went at full gallop around the round pen. Just like Monty said he would.

Flight.

I kept my eyes on his eyes, just as a predator would. Cash would run for roughly a quarter of a mile, just as horses do in the wild, before he would offer his first signal. Did he actually think I was a predator, or did he know he was being tested?

I believe it's somewhere in between, a sort of leveling of the playing field. A starting from scratch with something he knows ever so well. Predators and flight. A simulation, if you will. Certainly, he was into it. His eyes were wide, his nostrils flared. At the very least he wasn't sure about me, and those fifty-five million years of genetics were telling him to flee.

It was those same genetics that caused him to offer the first signal. His inside ear turned and locked on me, again as Monty had predicted. He had run the quarter of a mile that usually preserves him from most predators, and I was still there, but not really seeming very predatory. So now, instead of pure reactive flight, he was getting curious. Beginning to think about it. Maybe he was even a bit confused. Horses have two nearly separate brains. Some say one is the reactive brain and the other is the thinking brain. Whether or not that's true physiologically, emotionally, it's a good analogy. When they're operating from the reactive side, the rule of thumb is to stand clear until you can get them thinking. Cash was now shifting. He was beginning to think. Hmm, maybe this human is not a predator after all. I'll just keep an ear out for a bit. See what happens.

Meanwhile, my eyes were still on his eyes, my shoulders square, and I was still tossing the line behind him.

Before long, he began to lick and chew. Signal number two. I think maybe it's safe to relax. I think, just maybe, this guy's okay. I mean, if he really wanted to hurt me, he's had plenty of time, right?

And, of course, he was right. But, still, I kept up the pressure. Kept him running. Waiting for the next signal.

It came quickly. He lowered his head, almost to the ground, and began to narrow the circle. Signal number three. I'll look submissive, try to get closer, see what happens. I think this guy might be a good leader. We should discuss it.

He was still loping, but slower now. Definitely wanting to negotiate. That's when I was supposed to take my eyes off him, turn away, and lower my head and shoulders. No longer predatorial, but assuming a submissive stance of my own, saying Okay, if it's your desire, come on in. I'm not going to hurt you. But the choice is yours.

The moment of truth. Would he, in fact, do that? Would he make the decision, totally on his own, to come to me? I took a deep breath and turned away.

He came to a halt and stood somewhere behind me.

The seconds seemed like hours.

"Don't look back," Monty had warned. "Just stare at the ground."

A tiny spider was crawling across my new Boot Barn boot. The collar of my jacket was tickling the hairs on the back of my neck. And my heart was pounding. Then a puff of warm, moist air brushed my ear. My heart skipped a beat. He was really close. Then I felt his nose on my shoulder... the moment of Join-Up. I couldn't believe it. Tears came out of nowhere and streamed down my cheeks. I had spoken to him in his own language, and he had listened... and he had chosen to be with me. He had said, I trust you.

At that moment everything changed.

Everything.

He was no longer my horse. I wasn't his owner. The first line of the movie, Hildago, said it right. Cash was now my little brother.

And what a difference he has made as this newcomer stumbled his way through the learning process. Cash never stopped trying, never stopped listening, never stopped giving.

I promised him that day that he would have the best life I could possibly give him.

The problem was I didn't know what that was.

But no stone would be left unturned because I now cared deeply about this horse, and I would be asking everywhere I went how do I make his life better. Not how do I make my life better. My life would get better when his did. And with that perspective it soon became very clear that there were things in his life that needed to get better. If what I was being told did not appear to be in the best interest of this horse who had trusted me and chosen me, then I didn't listen. I dug out the truth for myself. Because I now had the passion to drive me through the barriers. And to withstand the onslaught from those who did not seem to care about their horses as much as I did.

The day before all this we didn't have a horse or a clue. Today, after a great deal of study and research, we have finally chipped away at our cluelessness. And we're still learning every single day. We have eight horses and enjoy amazing relationships with them all. They live out 24/7, are healthy, happy and come whenever they're called by name. They have none of the diseases, ills, or behavior vices that plague so many horses today. Their diets consist of what they are genetically designed to eat. We play and work with them completely at liberty, almost never resorting to the use of halters and lead ropes.

In short, I cannot imagine how it could be any better. For us, or the horses. The horses who have changed the lives of so many thousands of other horses around the planet through our books, blogs, websites, and videos.

And I thank God for that every day of my life.

And for Cash.

Because every bit of it is his fault.

ॐ

Horses Don't Lie

It's funny when you start challenging tradition and people turn away from you. You want to stop and just be like the pack, but you can't! My questions included, "Why are some horses' ears pinned back all the time? Why does this horse crib, swish his tail, stomp, seem so despondent, run off with riders, bite, kick, etc.?" And then when I developed a further discerning eye, I wondered, "Why is one side of the shoulder bigger than the other? Why is the coronet band higher on one side of the hoof than the other? Why don't they get their shoes replaced for over 10 to 12 weeks? Why do they move so stiffly? Why don't they appear fluid and comfortable? Why don't they shed out uniformly in spring? Why do they have 'guard hairs' in the summer months?" No one wanted to answer these questions.

Keys to a Horse's Health

Horses have been on the planet, roaming the earth in the form of equus for over 50 million years. If they had the problems our domesticated horses have, they never would have survived all those years in the wild.

Horses don't have a design problem. This is the issue that was plaguing me for so long when I initially started learning about horses. I started thinking more and more about horses in the wild and how they have survived millions of years. I began to wonder if it is something that we have done to horses that caused all these problems. So what's the difference between wild horses and some of the things our domestic horses are exposed to?

12

LIVING IN TWO DIFFERENT WORLDS

In many ways we have yet to uncover the true nature of equus. You know that horses will show their true selves to you. Now you have to be willing to use your senses and intuition to connect with them and learn to recognize the messages they are sharing. However, just as you may have presumed your horse's intentions to be like some humans—maybe a little manipulative or less than honest—your horse may apply his experiences in the animal kingdom to you. You are a predator.

This has very little to do with your true intentions; it is your role in his natural world. Horses can be wary of us, especially if the relationship is new, and sometimes even when it isn't. If they're afraid or unsure, they will be on guard and react out of fear and for survival rather than as the loving, gentle awe-inspiring creatures they are. So what can you do? Understand the differences between predator and prey and change your behaviors accordingly to create a safe, open environment where both you and your horse can be more vulnerable. It is about stripping away assumptions and being honest about intentions and the very heart of being—for both you and your horse.

When interacting with your horse, be aware of the behaviors and the very nature of your presence that he may perceive as predator-like. Consider what alternative behaviors might be less threatening. Some of the things that imply our predatory nature are things we can't help, such as the placement of our eyes. We humans are predators and as such our eyes are placed at the front of our heads for sharp, focused sight. The eyes of prey animals are on either side of their head so that they can consistently keep a 360-degree lookout for danger. Your horse can see almost completely around himself, save for a tiny blind spot almost directly behind him, which is corrected by a slight turn. You can't change the placement of your eyes, but be aware that your horse has noticed them. Similarly, the placement of our ears is that of a predator, laid back and flat against our heads. And then we smile, which in the animal world could signify an animal ready to attack—ears flat, teeth bared. I have heard that this is why horses like cowboy hats. The turned up rim of a cowboy hat gives the appearance of straight-up, forward-facing ears like those of a prey animal. They give a sense of comfort and make us less threatening at first sight. I don't know that for sure, but it could be so.

There is a difference in the walk and approach of prey and predator. As predators, we walk in a direct line with purpose, straight ahead to our destination. When we approach a horse directly, it is perceived as if we are coming at him. Horses don't like to walk in a straight line if left to their own devices. They amble along a bit unpredictably. Given free rein they wouldn't walk down the road in a straight line, they would saunter from one side to the other. This tactic allows them to be more aware of their surroundings and puts them in a position to pivot, turn and go in the opposite direction quickly.

One simple thing we may do to be less menacing is to change our walk. Don't walk directly at your horse. Zigzag a bit, veering to the left or right as you make a casual approach. Horse expert Monty Roberts suggested what he calls "join up."

Joining up is when you get your horse to follow you. You turn your back to him or your shoulders to him. This demonstrates vulnerability and implies you're part of the team or herd. When Monty executes a join up, he walks in the opposite direction of the horse with his shoulder to the horse. That invites the horse to follow him.

My absolute favorite story is of **Monty Roberts and Shy Boy**.

Monty befriends a mustang and gets him to take a saddle and rider on his back in the wild. He then takes the wild horse, Shy Boy, with him back to his ranch and then around the country to show folks how being gentle, respectful and understanding is the best way to be with a horse.

Then later, Monty wonders whether Shy Boy would choose to be with him or back in the wild with a herd, so Monty takes him back out. After a night with the herd and considerable confusion, Shy Boy decides he would rather live his life with the kind and trustworthy human, Monty Roberts, rather than returning to his horse herd.

Every time I think of this story, I cry.

For prey animals to survive, everything about a predator holds significance. Even your teeth can be menacing. Has a dog ever bared his teeth at you? He's usually growling as well. It can be very scary. Teeth baring is a sign of being poised for battle or on the brink of attack in the animal world. Our human world dictates this behavior as a smile, a way to show joy and pleasure. When you approach your horse all smiley because you are happy to see him, he has to push past his primitive response of fear and desire to flee. Instead, try to have a joyful tone to your voice, even smile with your mouth closed to convey the same sense of happiness when greeting your horse.

Similarly, be cognizant of how your horse reacts to where you touch him. I had a horse that was extremely sensitive to being patted at the base of her neck, just above her chest. I love that area because it feels soft, warm and fleshy, but when I thought about it, I realized that it is that spot where a predator could come in for a fatal mouthful.

Also, note how you may smell to your horse. As an animal, he has a finely tuned sense of smell. If you eat meat, your horse can smell it on you. I'm not suggesting you become a vegan to please your horse, but just be aware of what he is going to sense from you.

Perception is Reality

While your horse will get to know you and the pure integrity and honest place of love from which you interact with him, as an animal of prey, he can't help but have a genuine place of fear and wariness. Imagine how your horse may feel—especially if it is a new relationship—if you briskly walk straight at him to pat him on the chest with a huge smile on your face, not wearing a hat and having just come from a barbeque dinner. Think about scenes from National Geographic, like a lion attacking a wildebeest in the bush! Be aware of the differences between prey and predator. While our horses may not be in a wild environment, they are still innately prey animals. We need to present our safe intentions with truth and integrity to create a symbiotic relationship with our horses.

Our Inherent Predatory Nature

Be aware of your inherent predatory nature and realize that it, too, is no longer necessary in our domestic environment, just as your horse is no longer required to flee from danger. And although humanity, in general, has a predatory nature, as a subsection, women can be seen as prey animals while men are predators. It is my belief that this is the reason women resonate with a symbiotic frequency to our horses. We can be more intuitive, more cautious and generally have a greater sensitivity.

All Work and No Play

Just as play contributes to a well-rounded personality, so it helps create a well-rounded relationship for you and your horse. If you're always asking your horse to work for you and making demands of him, then you have that relationship alone. By integrating play, and at liberty interactions, you expand the integrity of the relationship beyond the master versus servant role. You always need to be safe and in charge, but you can do that while at play. If you can play and give your horse more control, allowing him to be around you at liberty, you open your relationship to being more fully present. In his book, *Liberated Horsemanship: Breaking Bonds of Tradition*, Dr. Bruce Nock shares how you can engage your horse in playful ways. I have also seen people encouraging their horses to play with big balls, designed like big soccer balls. I haven't tried them, because at my place I think they would just get stuck in the fences or lodged in the trees, but I have seen videos and these huge balls look like a lot of fun for your horse to kick around the paddock, with or without, your participation. There is a lot of joy in playing with your horse in subtle, at liberty ways, versus by command and demand. If you can control your horse when he is at liberty, then you will be safer when you are working, riding, or in the ring with him.

At Liberty

I've had mixed reactions from people when I've suggested free autonomous interactions with horses. Some people are afraid to give up control, while others take it too far and release all control and responsibility. Think of it as being a parent of teenagers, when your kids are old enough to be out of your sight and go do things on their own. Allowing them to do things on their own creates and enhances the trust between you. If you do it in balance you don't lose parental authority and respect—you let go of some control and in the long run gain respect. In the same way, loosening the tight grip of a domineering working relationship with your horse may lessen control but not authority, while enhancing the trust and integrity of the relationship you have with your horse.

People may be hesitant to allow their horse too much freedom because they have a fear of him or for him. Parents fear that kids will make bad decisions when on their own, but that is the way they will learn. In both cases you always want to ensure safety measures are in place, but hopefully, the benefits of creating freedom outweigh the fear. Kids don't need you to be their friend. They need you to be the parent. Horses don't need you to be another horse for play, but a benevolent leader.

Sometimes when I haven't been able to ride for a while, I'll just pick up the lunge whip and saunter over to my horses, clucking. The intention is not really to chase them, but more to encourage some movement. If they are ready to run, they're off! Recently, after doing nothing for two weeks, one of my horses ran directly into the arena and lunged herself—at liberty. Tail straight in the air, she performed her rollbacks, circles, and flat out gallops. I love this expression of freedom!

There are some fabulous new methods emerging in our industry on training with horses at liberty. This means no halters, lines or attachments—just you and your horse playing. And your ability to make your wishes understood by your horse is a direct result of your level of understanding of your horse. There's no better feeling than to know your horse is with you because he wants to be. His natural inclination is really to go eat and be with the herd, but if he is choosing to play with you, run around in a circle and follow your lead, you have truly bonded.

I have been watching some fabulous trainers at events like Equitana, Road to The Horse and Equine Affaire. I love the Australians, Guy McLean and The Double Dans. And then of course, there's the magnificent Cavalia, by Cirque du Soleil. Of course, it's not all comfort and ease during these equine presentations.

It's one thing to allow movement at liberty and quite another to see a horse move free, free of tension and discomfort. Some of these colt-starting competitions are very stressful for the youngsters. It begins when they are herded into a trailer, leave their homes, embark on a strange, long bumpy ride confined in a box and ultimately end up in an arena with crowds of noisy humans all around them. Then a human stranger starts putting some serious pressure on them, and they must struggle to understand what's wanted of them. Their muscles tense. They are on alert. They really want to flee, but there's nowhere to go. There are fences and weird equipment around them. And then the saddle. It's actually heavy, and that alone hurts. This piece of restrictive equipment precedes the worse ones that are to come.

ɛɔ

My friend Guy McLean's beautiful understanding of starting young horses is combined with creative expression. The last time I heard him recite at Road to The Horse, there was not a dry eye in the house. Here is one example of his lovely poetry.

The Horseman's Promise

By Guy McLean

I promise I will see you
For all you were born to be
Before the training starts
Before the A's and B's

For I do not want to change you
Your heart, your soul, your spirit
For I want for you to sing your song
For the entire world to hear it

There will be many things to learn
For my world is different unto yours
And I will teach you with compassion
To understand the greater cause

For alone, you are quite special
Already perfect in nature's eye
But with my help, you'll be a diamond
That will brighten up the sky

I promise you I will be fair
Whilst you learn to understand

My requests will all be justified
I promise you a gentle hand

You will learn to seek my guidance
On pure knowledge you will feed
And I hope to share a bond with you
To fulfill both our needs

For a Horseman with no horse
Is just a man without a cause
And we will learn and grow together
To accept and know each other's flaws

I promise I will give my best
In every single moment
For you to give your best as well
Is to know your gift and own it

So whether your name is 'My Mates Cat'
Or 'Nugget', or 'Hope' or 'Thomas'
I will see you for all that you can be
For you have my 'Horseman's Promise'.

13

SADDLES & RIDERS

An obvious difference between a domestic horse and a wild horse is that domestic horses are saddled and ridden. I started looking at domestic horses and their back problems, and I noticed that most riders are unbalanced and that most saddles don't fit well. Our horses compensate for this as best they can, even contorting their bodies to try to balance the uneven load. Over the course of their lives, this results in horses with uneven shoulders and back problems.

Just as in human bodies, misalignment can cause other problems for horses. A horse's back is one of the two major hotspots for pain and problems in domestic horses.

Saddle Balance

Many back problems in horses stem from being ridden with unbalanced riders and saddles. The horse is most comfortable when the weight on his back is evenly balanced.

Very often, riders aren't symmetrical, and they're not evenly balanced from side to side. I know I'm not.

— Saddles are also often asymmetrical. Like a pair of human shoes, even good saddles may have slightly uneven construction.

— Bars may be placed unevenly.

— Panels may be stuffed unevenly, displacing the gullet or creating lumps or bumps.

— Wool flocking and padding changes shape over time.

If you hold your saddle upside down and put a straight edge down the center, you're going to notice a discrepancy from side to side. They come out of the factory like this, and if they don't start out uneven, they develop asymmetry over time, due to weather, wear and use changes.

When the rider's weight is not centered over the horse, the horse is going to try to compensate. Before I knew much about saddles, I accepted that my horse, Slash, carried his tail to the side simply because it was his way of going, his conformation—just the way it was. Then I recognized that he was actually contorting himself to stay under the weight of the saddle and rider because the saddle had a twist that shifted the load over to one side. When we got a new saddle, he straightened out

It's amazing how these problems take shape. In fact, if you look down the midline of most horses, you're going to find uneven development of the shoulders. Even without asymmetrical riders, horses (like humans!) may develop differently on the left and right sides of their bodies.

At Cavallo, we did a study on this several years ago, and we found that 80 percent of horses aren't balanced in the shoulder area. Typically, the muscle sling supporting the rib cage will also be asymmetrical.

Bodies also change and develop. A horse's musculature will change throughout the riding day as the horse tires, and over the season as the horse ages, develops, tones, or loses muscle mass.

Your horse is a living, dynamic creature, while a saddle is a static object. Even slight changes in your horse's weight throughout the year can have a significant impact on the saddle's fit. And naturally, saddle fit significantly impacts your horse's experience.

This may seem like common sense, but many riders forget that a horse normally undergoes alterations in weight and posture throughout the seasons and throughout his life. Despite these changes, we continue to put the same old saddles on their backs, year in and year out. You may have a custom saddle built for your horse, but with the horse's movement and your movement, things can skew over time.

Saddle Pads

Saddle pads can help somewhat, but most saddle pads under- perform when it comes to a customized and continually changing fit. You need to take all those dynamic movement situations into account. You want your saddle pad to create symmetry and a more even balance under your horse's saddle and under your weight.

For your horse's best health, you need to find a saddle pad that addresses all the changes that come with new seasons, age, injuries, and activities. And, at various points, you should have a qualified saddle fitter look at your saddle and evaluate whether changes are needed to prevent back problems and pain for your horse. Saddle pads do help with saddle fit, back issues, and all the other things that go along with riding on horses' backs, and I have witnessed great success when horses are provided with the comfort of Cavallo pads—but as you are surely aware, it's not the whole picture.

14

SHIFTING THROUGH CHANGE

When I first thought about the title of this chapter I was thinking about how caring for a horse is a profound responsibility. You're wholly responsible for their care—similar to the responsibility of raising a child. One of many challenges is the sheer quantity of conflicting advice, pointing in all directions. Neither a child nor a horse comes with an owner's manual; however, there is no shortage of data, books, and information available to direct and advise you.

It is our job as horse owners (as parents) to sift through it all, find what works for us, matches our beliefs and is right for our horse (or child). It can be difficult to choose a course of action when everything you hear comes from seemingly expert, but conflicting sources.

Functional Hoof Conference

In 2010, I spoke at the Functional Hoof Conference at Werribee Veterinary Hospital just outside Melbourne, Australia. There were a lot of well-known speakers in attendance, including Dr. Robert Bowker and Professor Chris Politt, who are professional veterinarians specializing in hooves.

I listened to both of these experts, and they did not agree on how the hoof falls, the function of the strike of the hoof on the ground, or even how it strikes—either by making contact with the heel and rolling over to the toe—or if it was more like a ski boot, plunk on the ground all at the same time and lift all at the same time. Conflicting viewpoints substantiated make it hard for the layperson to be able to differentiate and determine what is truly best. Horses can also be different in how they walk, their movements, structure, if they are shod or barefoot, etc. Our industry is dogmatic, opinionated and inconclusive. The responsibility lies on us to sift through the mire of what we believe to be true and come up with what is really appropriate for the well-being of our horse and for ourselves.

I would encourage you to own the decisions you make for your horse. Too often things remain the same even if they are wrong because no one wants to step up and change. Take responsibility by following your gut. Soak up as much information as possible. Ask questions and then trust your intuition.

As president of Cavallo, one of the most interesting parts of my job is to hear the personal stories people share about their experience with their horse's hooves. The process of transitioning from shod to barefoot is fraught with a variety of emotions and growing pains. These tales, ranging from funny to tragic, all have a common thread. It is a story of challenge, of leaving the old behind and stepping into a field of the unknown.

The possibilities are endless, and without restraint our minds present an incessant array of "what ifs." What if my horse becomes irreparably lame? What if I offend my farrier and then he won't come back when I need him? And so on. Rest assured; you are not alone. To make change, we have all gone down a version of this frightening path.

An Epiphany

I'll never forget the fateful morning when I just sat down in the field with my horses to ponder, yet again, their hooves. The sky was as tumultuous as my thoughts. Shards of the sun were piercing through fast ominous clouds. As my mind struggled to make sense of it all, to gain some clarity, I finally grasped that the problem could not be the hoof intrinsically, not God's magnificent creation. The problem was our treatment of those hooves, the archaic practice of nailing metal shoes into their feet! Looking at the metal shoes, the nails, the pounding, the concussion, led me to ask, "Why? Why do we do it? Why can't the hoof be free?"

On that very day, I pulled the metal shoes off my horse's feet and vowed to never nail them on again. I freed my horse.

Now I had several new issues, one in particular with my farrier. I asked him to take the metal shoes off and trim the horses hooves to be natural and barefoot. Do you think I was met with resistance? Absolutely. "You need metal shoes to protect their feet. You cannot ride a barefoot horse. We have bred the good hoof out of them. They are domesticated and can't be barefoot." The objections went on and on.

Breaking Up is Hard to Do

We, along with our farrier, are responsible for our horses' health and well-being. We have some tough decisions to make in many cases, especially when we ask our long-time-family-friend farrier to take off the metal shoes, and he refuses. I empathize with how difficult it can be to go against the grain. Believe me, I've been there. You may have to disconnect with one of your key horse-life relationships—it's like breaking up with your hairdresser or even your husband.

So my advice is to lovingly meet your farrier face to face. Tell him you are taking over control of your horse. Thank him for everything and let him know that his services will no longer be required. Or you could sit down and lovingly write a "Dear John" letter and send it by mail. If you just can't be that personal, in this electronic day and age, you have the option of email or text message. If necessary, call him and leave a voicemail when you know he's away. You could deploy any number of break-up strategies. However, as we all have experienced, or wish we had experienced in our love lives, especially when we are the ones left behind, it is nice to know why. Quite honestly, I think we are responsible for helping to spread the word that there is a better way—you and hundreds of thousands of others are choosing better, healthier practices for the holistic well-being of your horse, which includes ditching the metal shoes.

Taking care of a horse is a profound responsibility. You have to trust your gut, be honest, stand in integrity, and take control. Take your power. Be non-negotiable about getting your requests met. Do not waver from your beliefs about what is right and know that you deserve the best love and care. Commit to living what is true—for both yourself and for your horse.

Don the Farrier

Don was the first farrier I had contact with when I started my involvement with horses over twenty years ago. Meeting Don was like meeting the savior who would spare my horse from getting all those horrible afflictions that seemed so confusing to me then as a new horse owner. I believed that it was he who could keep my horse from the dreaded navicular syndrome, contracted heels, thrush, and all that awful stuff. So, Don was like a god to me. He was tough looking and always just a bit disheveled, like he had just come from a tousle. He had an air about him as if he knew something no one else knew. I imagined he had just come from starting a feisty colt or that he was so creatively genius he forgot to do the mundane that day, like shave or comb his hair. He was a different species in a way, one that I revered for its wild, raw simplicity. Here was a man's man.

I remember getting tongue tied. Honestly, I am a woman with a university education, and I couldn't speak. He had this sort of drawl and cowboy talk like "y'all" and "howdy." I had no idea who this person was, but I knew I must embrace him. At first when with Don, I felt confused and vulnerable. He would walk around my Rocky, hem and haw, appear extremely important and then get to work with Big Man tools, grunting and groaning and clanking metal to the hissing fire of his forge. It was truly awesome and inspired my respect until I began to understand the procedure, do my homework and ask the pertinent questions.

That's when skepticism replaced esteem.

If Don would have at least tried to answer my line of questioning with anything more than patronizing me, I may have backed off. What he said was, "Carole, this is man's work. You leave this business of the horse's feet to me. You just get your butt in the saddle and ride." I was insulted. How dare he refer to my butt anyway, and what in the world does that have to do with keeping my horse sound? It became obvious that this cowboy was less than the image I held up. His was not the answer I was looking for.

My education progressed in earnest when I realized that I had to find my own answers. Sometimes there is just no easy way. This was quite some time ago, when we did not have the benefit of all the information now available online. The controversial Dr. Hiltrud Strasser from Germany attracted me. Yet even after reading her $700 textbook twice, it was more scientific data than I could absorb. Initially, it all made me feel like my mind was soft and mushy—like scrambled eggs. Maybe I should just get in the saddle and ride. Forget all this stuff. Sometimes though, when you open a door there is just no turning back. I attended seminars, leg and hoof dissections, and joined and promoted communities of like-minded advocates. I did, indeed, get the basics I required to confirm that my line of questioning was valid.

My knowledge grew in proportion to the scrutiny which I viewed Don's work. Big "wows" in the hairline with one side higher and stronger than the other resulted in more off one side of the hoof than the other all the way around. But when comparing the opposite sides, they were imbalanced, but symmetrically so. I asked Don, "What about the under-slung heels?" He replied, "Oh, we'll fix those by extending the metal shoes behind so that the heels grow into them." (Yeah, right.) "Contracted heels?" He countered that by saying, "Oh, we'll just widen the shoes a smidge." (As if a ½ cm would make a difference.) "What if a shoe falls off?" "We'll just put eight nails in and make sure the last ones are right at the back."

I would complain, "But Don, it's not working. My horse still has contraction, is under slung, imbalanced, and moves stiffly."

Don's patronizing response was always, "You just can't see the positive changes. This was all created by the last farrier and takes some time to fix. Your horse is happy. Get your butt in the saddle and ride." Nothing changes. I was so frustrated that he was not listening to me and not taking my comments seriously that I wanted to take that farriers' rasp and just shave off a little arrogant bravado.

When I left that barn, I left Don behind. Although it was not comfortable, I appreciated the experience, because not only did I leave Don behind, I graduated from that stereotype conditioning. The thing is I didn't start out with a very high level of self-esteem. I never really felt smart enough, pretty enough, or successful enough, so I took a little abuse here and there. I accept that I may have even co-created it in a way by my demeanor. But it stopped there. This experience with Don was a big turning point for me, and since then I no longer accept condescension. I no longer accept being patronized or demeaned.

Looking back, I can hardly believe I took it as long as I did.

It wasn't just that my Rocky had extraordinary problems. I went on to own four more horses that I could not keep 100 percent sound all the time and whose hooves rarely looked good enough to my developing, discerning eye. You know how it goes: In an effort to improve we change farriers, experiment with various feed programs, give the horses time off, try different exercise programs, but all with inconsistent results. I could not believe that lameness was just a part of the horse's life. Why would such an amazing structure be inherently flawed? How could these beautiful animals be doomed to consistent hoof ailments? Involvement in the care of horses' hooves is an issue that responsible horse owners can no longer delegate away.

The Natural Nature of Horses

We now know wild horses move a lot of the time. They scavenge and live on scrubby grasses. They don't wear blankets to stay warm; they use their muscles. They hydrate their feet when they drink. Above all, they run—barefoot.

There's some discrepancy about how much wild horses move, but it's anywhere from eight to twenty miles a day, running with the herd and foraging for food. As they run, they naturally trim their hooves. With each step, the hoof mechanism pumps blood, providing a flow of nutrients into all the coriums to keep the hoof tissue healthy and help the horse survive.

We can give our horses their best, healthiest lives by reproducing these conditions as much as is practical for them and for us.

15

THE WOOLLY MAMMOTH IS NOT CHASING YOU

In the wild, horses have access to hours of grazing, which not only trims their hooves, but also their teeth. Our domestic horses generally don't have that, so they need dental help. It's important to have a horse's teeth balanced (floated) periodically.

The problem occurs when practitioners get too heavy-handed. The industry has developed power tools to make it easier for practitioners to float horses' teeth. But power tools also make it easy to get carried away and shave too much off their teeth.

Unlike humans, horses' teeth continue to grow about three or four inches until they are around 12 years old. Some older horses develop serious problems masticating their food, because somewhere along the line, someone may have been a bit heavy handed with the power tools and shaved too much off their teeth.

I think of it like this: If our horses only grew three or four inches of hoof throughout their lifetimes, we'd be extremely careful who we let near them with a rasp or nippers. Similarly, we need to be very careful who we allow in our horses' mouths. When choosing a "dentist" for your horse, make sure the practitioner is well educated and uses hand tools.

Time For a Checkup ?

Intuition Not Chatter

They say you shouldn't judge a book by its cover. But isn't that something we all do? Our first impression of what we observe on the outside—both the physical and the behavioral—can give us important information about what may be happening on the inside of that being, be he a horse or a human. We form a snap judgment. However, with practice and self-awareness, that judgment can be based more accurately on true observation and a little intuition rather than stereotypes, which is true both for humans and horses.

It is difficult to observe from an intuitive place if your mind is full of chatter. It's a good idea to stop for a moment when you walk into the barn. Stand still and take a deep breath or two. It gets you to a place where you can lose the preoccupations of your day outside the barn—the business, family, the to-do list—and be present with and for your horses. Deep breathing is a way to move to a place of stillness and become more aware of what is around you. Just know that when you are with your horses, it is important that you recognize the opportunity to release every-thing else going on in your world and truly be with him. We want to cultivate a symbiotic relationship with our horses and get a sense of who they are, their personalities and needs. After all, we ask a lot of our horses, especially show animals. They deserve our undivided attention and to be tended to during our time together. This goes for our loved humans as well. The best thing we can do is really be present for them.

Even though we often anthropomorphize our horses, the reality is they can't talk to us. They communicate, but they can't talk. So we have to use our senses to build a relationship with them and understand what they are saying and showing us. It is also through our senses that we will detect and understand any physical issues or needs. It seems obvious that we use our senses to get closer to our horses, yet if you aren't actively paying attention, you'll miss something and lose out on that.

Duvets & Blankets (Rock the Baby)

The largest muscle mass in the horse's body lies just under the first layer of skin. This muscle mass activates when the horse is either cold or hot. As the muscle mass contracts, it lifts the hair follicles up off the horse's back.

Those hair follicles then act as a layer of insulation. If the horse is too hot, the muscle mass will contract to lift the hair follicles, allowing air to circulate and cool the horse. If the horse is too cold, the hair follicles lift to act as a natural blanket for the horse.

That's how wild horses control their temperature, but what happens with our horses? We put blankets on them, so this muscle mass doesn't get activated. By keeping our horses from ever getting cold, we ensure that this natural response system in the horse lies dormant. This practice can actually deplete the immune system of your horse.

So why do we blanket our horses? We do it because it makes us feel better. We feel comfortable when we go to bed at night and our horses are within the confines of nice warm stalls with cozy blankets. It's easy to get carried away and forget that horses are not people. They're wild animals—they have a layer of fur, and their skin is more of a hide. They don't need to be coddled in a duvet all the time.

Don't get me wrong, I'm not saying don't blanket. You'll know intuitively when it's right to blanket. What I'm saying is you don't need to buy into the marketing hype or cover your horse with blankets in fashion colors all year long. Every year the blanket companies develop new trends and accessories. It's no different than the human fashion industry, shaking things up with the next hot thing each season, whether we need it or not.

Lead a Horse to Water

Another difference between domestic and wild horses is what happens when horses drink. Water is so incredibly important, isn't it? It's important to the immune system, the liver, and to the kidneys to flush out toxins.

As it turns out, it's important to the feet as well. When horses in the wild go to hydrate, they actually stand in watering holes. While they're drinking and quenching thirst internally, they're also hydrating their feet, creating elasticity and nourishing their hooves with water. Domesticated horses often drink out of buckets or troughs, so they don't normally get the opportunity to do this.

Locked in the Bathroom

Stalls are not good places to keep horses. Some horses stay in their stalls for days on end. That's very sad because horses are herd animals. They love to be together and engage in their equus language, touching, feeling, and bossing each other around in the pecking order. Locked in stalls, the natural order doesn't exist. They don't even get to move. If someone doesn't believe this is a problem, I say, "Go and stand in your bathroom. Close the door and just stand there. Nowhere to go. No one to talk to. Nothing to do. Are you happy in your bathroom? And you only have two legs."

When I think about physical protection for my horse I consider how she needs a safe, adequately spacious, clean and dry shelter for protection. We can easily get caught up in the glamour of building these big, plush, beautiful stables with all the bells and whistles. They can be more posh and well equipped than some homes for humans. However, when it comes to shelter, all your horse really needs is cover from the rain and refuge from the wind with clean, dry hay. Although stalls are great shelter, they're just shelter for your horse, not a place to store him. When stored in a stall for too long, your horse feels sad, bored, lonely, forgotten, and stressed out. A horse in this situation can develop a disorder called "learned helplessness," which happens when the horse feels he has no control to change or alter the circumstances of his life, and further, that any step he might make results in unwanted results. This is a precursor to what some refer to as the silent epidemic of equine depression.

"Care and not fine stables maketh the horse."

- Danish proverb

Living Environment, Protection, and Zoos

We cannot ignore that our domestic animals are animals in captivity. They generally have far less space than they would in a natural environment, and far too often that space is less than desired or adequate. Studies have shown that horses stalled for extended periods of time display increased symptoms of stress and dysfunctional behavior like cribbing, stomping, and weaving. For the most part, they do not have control over their own continued existence—running from danger, finding food, mating for propagation of the species, etc. Survival depends on the ability to make the correct choices. Yet our domestic horses—our friends—receive their food, get brushed, and are exercised all at our hands. They have little say in the matter. This lack of control and independence in their living conditions and environments can have a mental or emotional impact that can shorten their lifespan if not considered by their human caretakers— by you and me.

Look at polar bears, for example. When kept in zoos they have a 65 percent infant mortality rate. Wild elephants live for about 56 years, but captive ones have an average lifespan of 17 years.

Freedom of Choice

This is not to say we should not keep our horses, but just be aware of their innate desire to have some control over their environments. They want a sense of freedom as much as you and I do. My horse, Slash, loves to open gates. It makes him feel really smart. So we have two gates on the property that he can open which do not allow escape, but that's not his agenda anyway. Sometimes it takes him all day to open the gate, and he just goes and stands on the other side and acts very proud of himself. You can tell he has a sense of achievement for doing it. It helps him feel like he is in control.

A Horse is a Horse

The Greek word, anthropomorphism, was first used in the 1700s, mostly for storytelling and animal lore. It is the process of bestowing human characteristics on animals. And we do it to our horses. All the time.

Don't try to make him human. Understand the beauty of his pure, limitless nature. He doesn't judge, he just is. It's the beauty of simplicity, balance and the silence in which all things are possible. He is peaceful, and you can be, too. When you tap into your sensory perception, you are more like your horse. We tend to lose this as we grow up and learn to categorize and judge.

"There are children playing in the street who could solve some of my top problems in physics, because they have modes of sensory perception that I lost long ago."

- Robert Oppenheimer, 1904 – 1967

Horses Make Us Live Longer

Your restful awareness when you are with your horse can contribute to your overall sense of well-being and extend even when you are not with your horse. Several studies have shown that people with horses in their lives live longer, happier, healthier, and more joyful lives. We can be free of our past conditioning by embracing the beauty of equus, by embracing the present moments in time that we have with our horse. Forget that you are human, fraught with mortgages, truck payments, relationships, and appointments. For the time you are together with your horse, become more like him rather than trying to make him more like you.

Fight or Flight & Blood Platelets

Watch your horse when he feels threatened and afraid. Physiological changes happen instantaneously. His blood platelets become stickier so that his blood can clot easily in case of injury. His heart rate increases, the stress hormones increase and the blood shifts to the muscular structure so he can flee, which leaves less blood for the circulatory system. A real danger or threat does not occur with our domestic horses very often now, but their natural, wild "horsey" needs are not always met. Psychological stress can create the same type of anxiety for your horse. Being confined, stuck in a stall, overfed or malnourished or simply misunderstood as a prey animal can create the same fight or flight response, resulting in problems like cribbing, stomping, weaving, or digestive problems like diarrhea and colic. Infections have greater opportunity in a horse's stressful compromised state. Weakened immunity, circulation, and heart problems can all be a sign of our lack of understanding. Nailing metal shoes onto the bottom of their feet clearly inhibits natural hoof function. When their hooves are weakened, their natural flight response is compromised, and this is a great source of anxiety for many horses. It is our responsibility to our kept animals to emulate a more natural environment for them and to understand their innate flight response.

Presence, Connection & Senses

It isn't just for the sake of joy and full experience that you want to be aware of inherent nature. A sense of current awareness connects you to your horse at his level of awareness, which in turn reconnects you to your intuition. When you are present, your senses are heightened. This is important to survival. Your horse uses his keen senses to notice the scent of a mountain lion in the air, or a rustle in the bushes not perceptible to most human beings.

We humans, in a more primitive time, used to be more in tune with our senses and intuition when fight or flight was directly related to life or death. Now, with the security and safety we experience in the modern world, relatively speaking, our fight or flight nature is used when the adrenaline pumps because someone cut us off in traffic or we have to get a project finished by Thursday.

In fact the high stress, constant noise, chatter and overall colossal speed of life may fling us into fight or flight mode even more often than the occasional stalking woolly mammoth of slower, simpler times. Sure, we had to react to danger or challenges occasionally, but not six times a day. But even though we're not being hunted down, the impulse is innate, so when someone flips us the finger speeding by us in traffic, it appears confrontational, and we are provoked to fight mode. There goes our consciousness. But are we breathing? Are we present? Is this really how we want to behave?

16

MAJESTY THAT IS HORSE

Few animals, if any, can rival the majesty of the physical presence of a horse. Both his statuesque gentle strength when standing still and the rippling power shown at all levels of gait demonstrate the elegance of this creature we love. Just as the human body is designed to move and needs to be cared for and nurtured properly for good health, so does the horse. Do you ever feel elevated beyond human status when you're flying along with the freedom, power, and speed of your horse beneath you? It's like magic.

"A horse is the projection of peoples' dreams about themselves - strong, powerful, beautiful - and it has the capability of giving us escape from our mundane existence."

-Pam Brown

Exercise

The horse is an animal of prey. His survival mechanism is to flee. Running is part of a horse's very sense of well-being. He needs the ability to run. He needs space in which to run and good health to make him capable of running. Running keeps your horse fit better than any other exercise. The fitter and more capable a horse is to run, the happier he will be. However, rarely can you ride horses often and long enough to keep them at peak fitness. I know I struggle with this. We must provide them opportunities to exercise otherwise.

Creating an environment that encourages movement for your horse will support his fitness level. You may move his food to different parts of your land, requiring him to move throughout the space. You may put feed and water in separate locations to make him cover more ground throughout the day. If you have smaller acreage, you may consider creating alleyways or a labyrinth in the paddock.

Paddock Paradise

Jamie Jackson wrote about a concept called "paddock paradise" which creates a template method that enables you to redesign your property into pathways that have specific ground surfaces; he has a number of ideas for you to consider. Joe Camp also offers some creative solutions to navigating the paths and providing exercise as the horse makes his way to food and water. Sometimes you can shake up your horse's movement routine by introducing him to a different environment with other horses. He will have to establish a new pecking order and hunt for food, thereby increasing his exercise.

If you have a neighbor you can switch horses with from time to time; it can create some excitement in the pasture to make them move around. One thing I found helpful in setting up a paddock paradise is river rock or drainage rock. You want to make sure it's the right size—you don't want it so small that it would go up into any hoof separation that your horse might be experiencing. You just want a nice size to help the horse self-trim his own hooves and develop a healthy sole. You can put some drainage rock in different areas of your property, say between the water and the feed, where they'll have to walk over it.

Hydration

Another trick is to help the horses hydrate, especially in dry weather. As previously mentioned, most domestic horses drink water from buckets, so they don't have an opportunity to stand in a watering hole and hydrate their hooves the same way that wild horses do. When the weather is dry, you can hose down an area where the horses have to go for feed. Essentially, you are making a little mud puddle in which they can stand while eating so their hooves can hydrate.

Lunging

Riding is the best way to exercise your horse, as you know. The exercise methods I just mentioned provide variety, especially when you're not able to ride. If you don't have time to ride, or you're ill, or injured, you can exercise your horse by lunging. Lunging is an option for when your time is strained, as it is best to only do this for a short time. If you aren't familiar with it, lunging guides the horse in a circle at different gaits. Moving in a circle is more difficult than moving in a straight line, and therefore, a somewhat challenging exercise for your horse. Manage the size of the circle based on the abilities of your horse. The smaller the circle, the more difficult, therefore, a larger circle is better. This exercise is not recommended for very young horses.

Lunging can also be used as a repetitive exercise for muscle building, especially for circumstances such as treating a one-sided horse. Lunging, like any exercise, needs to be utilized only if your horse can physically handle it. The stressors on the legs can be a worry if your horse is not very fit. Be aware though that mindlessly going around in circles is probably not too much fun. You can get creative and engage with your horse by varying the speeds and directions through body language or word cues, making things more fun and interesting for both of you.

Your horse is an athlete and can do a lot more than many of us think. She needs regular exercise routines and opportunities, structured and unstructured. Like any good trainer, you should build in warm-up and cool-down phases into your horse's activities. Good training practices can prevent a lot of problems. Spending ten minutes at a walk to warm up will ensure that the horse's muscles are well supplied with blood. This gets the circulatory system activated with more oxygen being supplied to the muscles to enable them to work efficiently. You can cool down after a workout with a few rounds of a relaxed trot with a long and low neck position. This helps to ensure that the muscles relax and stay soft and supple.

Muscle Fitness

You should continuously assess the health and fitness levels of your horse. Exercise is critical, but over-stressing muscles during exercise can lead to injuries and trauma, such as tight, sore muscles, strains, or sprains of tendons and ligaments. These injuries are slow to heal and could cause your horse discomfort for months. As with people, age, a history of injuries and illness, and level of activity all contribute to determine much of a horse's well-being. You'll need to adjust your horse's exercise routine accordingly, taking all information into consideration, including how he responds to changes in activity. As he gets older, your horse will be less active, and he'll require a calmer, gentler life and movement routine. If you look and listen, your horse will tell you what he needs, what he wants and what he can and cannot do.

It is easy to get complacent with our health. We just accept that things are the way they are and that we're destined to be in pain. We may become so used to a discomfort that we hardly notice it anymore. Has that happened to you? As a yoga instructor, I see this frequently. Some people have compensated so much for some pain, past injury or discomfort that it has significantly altered their bodies. They come to do yoga, and they're not even aware that one side is quite stiff compared to the other. They do not realize how much pain, stress, and soreness they had been dealing with until it is gone.

I have a friend who had daily low-level headaches. She popped an Advil each morning and sometimes a second one each night, as if it were normal. It wasn't until she began seeing a chiropractor that she knew what it was like to be without pain.

The complacency we sometimes have about our health is not unlike how we treat our house. How many times have you gone up the stairs and not taken the basket of laundry or stack of books sitting on one of the stairs up with you? Or have you accepted that in order to open the pantry door you have to push the doorknob in while you turn it? We live with disorder day in and day out, yet when company is coming, or we are preparing the house for sale, we take time to notice the details and make the environment pleasant for someone else. Our lives are complex, and sometimes it is just easier to deal with a discomfort in your environment— or in your body—rather than take action to relieve it. Often, it isn't even a conscious effort—we simply don't notice the changes in our well-being because we are too busy working or worrying. The catch is that when you are not taking time to notice, to sense how you feel and nurture your state of wellness, you are not fully living.

17

SENSORY RELATIONSHIP

I've been talking about people, but the same is true for the well-being of your horse. That is why it is so important to build a sensory relationship with your horse and really get to know him through sight, touch, hearing, and smell. As you fine tune your senses and build that connection with him, you will be better able to know when his health and well-being are out of line. You will be in a better position to prevent discomfort or disease and certainly more capable of providing aid and relief at the onset of an issue. Most importantly, you will have a deeper relationship with him based on an intuitive trust and knowing.

Your Own Path

I'm not trying to diagnose your horse. My intent is to demonstrate a number of things you may notice—signs of illness or discomfort you can identify by sight, touch, hearing or smell. My hope is that if you build a sensory relationship with your horse you will be better equipped to notice when something is a little off and do something about it for the love and care you have for him. This last decade has seen the most dynamic change in horse keeping. The industry and owners are caring more about their horses' comfort. They are opening up and looking for ways of working with their horses. Gone are the days of breaking a horse—now you "start" a horse or "gentle" him, not break him. Both language and action are shifting. I hope this book contributes to a kinder, more holistic and intuitive approach in caring for horses. Each of us needs to soak up all the information possible and forge our own path.

This story from the book, *The Horses In My Life*, by my good friend Monty Roberts, is just one of the many stories that highlight how the personality of a horse can really shine through for someone who is prepared to listen.

℅

Johnny Tivio was, at the time, a quarter horse standing at stud on a major thoroughbred operation, and while thoroughbred people would think him inferior to their wonderful racehorses, Johnny was fully of the opinion that Flag Is Up Farms was his property and that he was fully in charge of the activities there. We were able to give him his own field during the day and a wonderful stable for the nighttime. He had his harem, and for a horse ten years of age, he could look forward to many years of contentment.

I rode Johnny often for the next seven or eight years, and while we worked cattle and surveyed the farm with regularity, there was never again the need to perform with the kind of intensity reserved for competition. Champion thoroughbred jockeys, Bill Shoemaker and Laffit Pincay, Jr., rode Johnny during the time of his retirement and never forgot their experience. My wife, Pat, would often ride Johnny while instructing our three children in the skills of horsemanship.

People often ask me if I think horses enjoy being ridden. I usually answer by saying that it depends on how the riding is done and who the rider is. I tell them about Johnny and about how certain I am that he enjoyed every minute of being ridden during his retirement time. You don't have to be a genius to see when a horse is having fun with his activity, and Johnny would tell you clearly that it was fun.

Johnny Tivio was with us until the end, and I think it is only fitting to leave this story while Johnny was alive and as happy as a horse could be. He made many trips during retirement with Pat and me to other ranches to gather cattle or ride through the mountains just for the fun of it. I have decided that I would like to reserve my last hours with Johnny as the conclusion of this book.

Johnny Tivio was appropriately the last horse I showed in serious competition. The creation of Flag Is Up Farms made necessary my retirement from the show ring. Somewhere, there must have been a force suggesting that this was a fitting way for me to end my career. If the lessons of Ginger, Brownie, and all the others to come before him did anything for me where Johnny was concerned, they were to teach me how to observe, respect, and stay out of his way.

Johnny helped me with every horse that followed him in a profound manner, and I could fill a hundred pages with the details of those lessons. It is easy to relate, however, that the most important piece of information that Johnny brought to me was that there was a time in his life when he was abused and forced. During this time he certainly didn't reach his full potential. When the environment was changed so there was request rather than demand, when there was love instead of abuse, he was able to perform like no other before him. Johnny Tivio is not just burned into the memory of Monty Roberts, but *he has made an indelible mark on hundreds of Western trainers and certainly on the very industry in which he performed.*

☙

I wrote earlier how to use your senses to really notice and care for your horse. Just having senses is a gift from God. What a blessing to touch, taste, smell, hear, and see all that we can. We often take these gifts for granted when we quickly gobble up a meal instead of savoring the flavors in each bite; when we're outside without taking the time to feel the textures of life, smelling the fresh grass and flowers, hearing the subtle wind and song of a bird. We live through our senses every day without really being aware of them. Make an effort to heighten your senses through awareness. Doing that will bring you to, and help you make the most of the present moment. It is in being present that we are most aligned with our intuition and can be guided by it in all we feel, think, say, and do.

We horse people are powerful independent thinkers, and our horses give us the strength to walk the talk and travel down the less trodden trail. We gravitate to ideas around natural, holistic health care for ourselves, our family and our horses. We do not adhere to doctrines just because they have always existed. We question. We seek. We want to know. And we are not afraid. We want to do the best we can by our horses. We owe them that for all they do for us.

Physiology

A horse is very sensitive to the slightest change in his environment, including that of the people and other animals around him. Horses can be triggered to run because of the micro movement of a shiver in the herd. Horses communicate in a variety of ways, both among themselves and with you. Most of your horse's communication is quite subtle, visually and aurally. These subtle physical signs will help you understand the health of your horse. For example, you'll want to see her bright eyes because the eyes show vitality, just as they do with people. If you notice clouding or a despondent nature, investigate or talk to your vet.

Subtle Signs of Stress

The condition of the coat can be a good indicator of health. If you are constantly blanketing your horse, then you may not always notice the natural condition of his coat. It should be shiny and sleek. I just love when one of my horses sheds out in the spring and unveils his gorgeous deep-amber dapples. Patching or unsmooth hair is not a good sign. Brushing stimulates circulation and will help the health of the horse and his coat. Watch for guard hairs, which are longer strands inconsistent with the rest of his coat. These can indicate poor internal health.

Your horse should stand square in the front with feet parallel. If they are not parallel, check his hooves. Other signs of discomfort, pain or injury in the hoof or leg may include holding his feet back rather than forward, shifting his weight a lot, refusing to let you pick up his feet, or a smell or heat emanating from the hooves. Is your horse getting enough movement? Maybe some toxins are coming out through an abscess. Talk to your vet or trimmer and know the two pillars of proper hoof function. Your trimmer should be well versed in the proper trim to facilitate blood circulation and shock absorption. Use hoof boots for relief even while not riding. Your horse may have other sources of pain or discomfort. Look for signs like a tail swishing more distinctly, more than just a swish to shoo away flies. Notice his ears; if they are pinned back he is likely in discomfort or angry.

Body Language & Five Senses

You may primarily use body language and words to direct your horse. But a two-way conversation includes the communication tools of four of the five senses: sight, touch, hearing, and smell. (Clearly, we're not using the fifth sense and tasting our horse.) Also, you certainly can't underestimate the power of intuition, the sixth sense. So what can you expect in sensory communication? What should you look for and how should you decipher what you're sensing?

Sight

When I look at my horses, I see gentle yet strong, beautiful animals that are part of my family. Taking care of my horses means paying attention to the details of their physical body and behavior. When I first approach my horse, I walk around him. I take note of what I see. Is his tail swishing? Can I tell if he is moving it out of playfulness or frustration? I check for peaked eyelids or guard hairs, which can indicate a level of discomfort or depleted immunity, respectively.

I see how he reacts when I enter the space and interact with him. Is he happy or agitated? I look at the state of his body. It is the little signs that can alert you to his discomfort. Is he relaxed or tense? Does his hair appear rough or smooth? There is a certain line in a horse's hair pattern that moves up from his haunches and across his lower abdomen. When that line is pronounced, or there is a visible tightness, you know his gut may not be digesting properly or there may be some bloating. It is also prudent to look around the area and examine the consistency and color of your horse's manure. A change in color, texture or consistency could be a sign of digestive or hydration issues. If the manure is too tight, your horse may need electrolytes, or you may need to give him salt to encourage him to drink more. If his stool is too loose or runny then he may have issues digesting his food, i.e. the hay may be too green or the feed may have drying agents in it. If your horse is experiencing diarrhea, it may mean that parasites are overrunning his system.

Above all, I look at his feet. Is he comfortable on them? Does he need a little tidy up? How is the last trim growing out?

As much you may love riding, it can also be enjoyable watching your horse run and play. Beyond the joy, watching your horse walk or run from a distance allows you the opportunity to observe his gait and the mechanical workings of his body. Does he seem to be favoring a leg? Is there a "hitch in his giddy-up," as the saying goes?

Sometimes you can see things from a distance that you might not notice if you are always walking beside him or riding. It is also easy to get used to how he walks or runs and not realize it is not entirely without some level of discomfort. It is similar to how you may have hurt your knee and favored it for such a long time that it became second nature. Any discomfort became the norm. It isn't until you meet up with a friend for lunch who says, "Why are you limping?" that you realize what you are doing and that you haven't truly healed.

I encourage you to watch your horse with fresh eyes. If something seems off, check his hooves and address any issues. Give him an experience of being barefoot and wearing hoof boots.

Also, if you notice a difference in how he runs with and without being saddled, maybe he needs more technically advanced and ergonomically correct saddle pads. Remember the therapeutic saddle pads I started making by hand so many years ago? They have evolved into what we now call Cavallo's Total Comfort System Saddle Pads (See Resources).

They will help with alignment and movement and will improve his ability and comfort when carrying you, his rider.

Touch

Much of the sensory relationship you have with your horse will be with sight and touch. You will get a sense of your relationship from how he responds to your touch. If he flinches and moves away, he is sending you a message. If he leans in to you, there is a message. Horses are tactile animals that like to touch and groom one another. Regular grooming is a way to connect and communicate. Brushing is excellent for your horse's circulation and hair follicle health. Also, as you're grooming him or just walking around him and patting him down as part of your hello ritual, run your hands across his body and pay attention to what you feel. Notice if you feel tightness or knots. If you do this often, you will become familiar with him, and you will know if something feels wrong or has changed.

His body is not unlike your own body. Becoming familiar with how you feel, literally touching your skin, allows you to know if you have a knot or a new mole, if your neck is out of alignment—you'll know if things have changed. This is why women are told to do monthly breast exams, so that they know what they're feeling and can recognize a change, sometimes leading to early detection of breast cancer.

If you are regularly intentionally touching your horse and do feel tightness, consider some relaxing massage for him. If you are concerned with lumps or anything out of the ordinary, consult your vet.

Most horses like to be touched, but not every horse wants to be touched in the same way. I'm sure you know this to be true about people in your life. Some are huggers and others won't even shake your hand. While, like people, horses have different levels of being "people persons," there can be reasons they shirk your touch. I've said previously that horses are ever-present, not living in the past or the future. However, they do learn and carry that forward. So if your horse was abused in the past, he may be hesitant when you reach out to touch him. Be extra gentle, be patient and let your physical connection build over time. You will have to take care to earn his trust.

Each animal is different in how they like to show affection. Slash and I have a special ritual. Every time we come back from a ride I have to stand there and turn my back to him. He puts his head down and rubs his forehead against my shoulder. He gives his whole face a really good scratch that way. He really enjoys it. I love it, too. He could give me a bop with his head that would send me flying, but he rubs nicely, giving us both soothing sensations.

Building the touch relationship with your horse is simply about being sympathetic with their bodies, trying different things and allowing them to touch you, too. Kids are particularly great at cozying up to their horses. You see them cuddling up and wanting to take their sleeping bag to the barn.

Sometimes people are afraid to allow their horses to touch them, concerned they may bite, kick or knock them down. All of that could happen, so of course you have to be aware and respectful of the reality that they are large animals who may bite and can cause harm. Yet, their nature is gentle, and sometimes they want to nuzzle and touch you, too. Be open and build that relationship.

Hearing

Just because your horse is, for the most part, silent doesn't mean you shouldn't talk to her. I have taken two different approaches with my horses. There was a time when I was silent because they were silent. I would go the barn or the paddock and be with them, spend time with them. I thought that because they were such feeling animals and the voice wasn't their natural way to communicate, that it would make sense to not speak. I wouldn't use my voice, and instead I would use my body to communicate.

While certainly I communicated with my horses by gestures, signals, touch and even looks, it didn't feel right to not speak. I began talking to my horses as I would to anyone, man or beast. Now my horses and I know each other really well. I go into the barn and start chatting away, and they respond by interacting and whinnying. They like being talked to, hearing my voice.

Initially, when my husband would go into the barn, he was loud and booming with his deeper voice and jolly Australian nature. At first I thought that's not the way to be around horses. I was judgmental and presumed that my calmer, quieter nature would be more comfortable for my horses. Yes, they responded to me, and then Greg would bound into the barn and call out to the horses in a hearty, robust voice, "G'day mate, how you travellin'?!"

I saw that they responded well to him, too. It was clear that they could see an authenticity in the way that he was coming to them, just as much as me. He was being himself, and they could hear it in his voice. Horses know if you're trying to be something you're not. Remember that as prey animals they are naturally adept to hear the slightest disturbance, the subtlest signs. Just as they can hear a far off rustle in the trees or over the ridge and know if it is a sign of danger, they can sense your intention in the tone of your voice, your footsteps, and the pace of your breath. As they get to know you, you also will learn your horse's sounds and get to know her whinnies, nickers and snorts. You'll become familiar and understand if she is communicating happiness, pain, agitation, or fear.

Children can pick up on communication in a more subtle way as well. They inherently know if there is a difference between what someone is saying verbally and what the actual truth is. Some kids can carry this ability on through their lives, but most of us lose it.

Smell

If someone is not a horse person, smell may be the first thing they notice when they enter the barn. They may not find it pleasant. Can you imagine? I think most horses have a sweet, sweet smell. I am used to going out to see my horses and giving them a big hug around the neck. I just drink in their warmth and smell. I love that smell. You either do or you don't, and horse people do.

Dot is a horse that came from a stressful showing background. She was a high performing horse under a lot of stress. She didn't smell as sweet as my other horses. I think it was part of her stressful nature. She was high strung and loved to run. Her energetic nature coupled with an unnatural lifestyle that kept her cooped up, along with high-stress trainers who were concerned with winning, just hadn't worked too well for her. I believe it changed her chemistry and her smell. It took a couple of years living and working with me before her scent changed. She now has that beautiful aroma that only intrinsic health and comfort allow. And Slash is a horse who always smells incredibly sweet. He came from a big, working ranch, a good natural environment. I wish I could bottle it and sell it, a warm musky moss, cinnamon sweet smell. I love to just nuzzle in and soak it up. Yum.

This concept goes both ways of course. If your life is sweet, balanced and happy, your horse, with his enhanced olfactory capabilities will welcome your scent. And of course, you know the reverse scenario. So it pays to keep yourself happy. If not for a better night's rest, a clean, bright eye and feeling fantastic, it even results in a better relationship with your horse.

As with the other senses, you need to know what the normal smells are for your horse. Nasty, spoiled smells could be coming from an abscess in his mouth or an infection in his ears. Depending on the situation you may be able to address it yourself, or you may need to call a vet. Pay special attention to his feet. Thrush is a common, tenacious and smelly infection with a very foul odor. Thrush involves the frog and the central lateral sulci. If your horse is suffering from this, the area should be cleaned out with an antiseptic and then protected from dirt and moisture, with extra effort made to keep the hoof dry. Depending on how bad the infestation is you may have to dive deep into sensitive tissue to really clean it out. It can be painful for your horse. Once it's clean, it should be treated with an antibacterial product. Be diligent about treating it daily, as thrush is very persistent. Cavallo Hoof boots can be very helpful for extra protection.

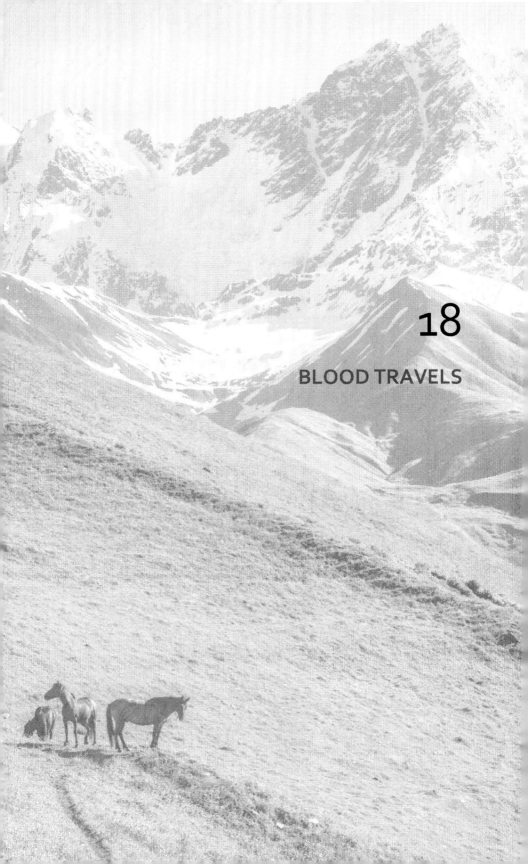

18

BLOOD TRAVELS

Wild horses run free. They move all the time. They're very active, and they run a lot—barefoot. Yet, we're told that our horses need metal shoes to be safe and protected. How can this be?

To understand, it's important to know a little more about how a horse's hooves work. You probably already know that when it comes to shoeing and hoof health, I learned the hard way to question traditional practices. I am going to tell you what I've learned so that you can benefit from my mistakes. My experience has led me to a passion about hoof health, so much so that it has become my life purpose to provide comfort and protection for horses.

Five Hearts and the Hoof Mechanism

The hoof is a miraculous structure, elegantly designed to support the horse's weight in movement. When a horse's weight descends with each step, the hoof is sandwiched between that load and the ground. Each time this happens, the hoof is designed to spread apart, allowing the coffin bone to drop like a trampoline. This is the natural shock-absorbing feature of the hoof—the walls spread up to six millimeters from side to side, and the sole draws flat.

Hoof care is critical. No hoof, no horse. You may have heard it said that a horse has five hearts: four on the ground and one in the chest. This refers to the frog's blood-pumping function, circulating blood down through the extremities and back again. The frog spreads the heel apart, drawing the sole flat and inviting the bone structure of the leg to descend into the hoof, absorbing shock. As it does, it pumps blood through all of these structures.

This is how shock is absorbed in the hoof capsule. If you can accept that circulation is imperative to the distribution of nutrients throughout the system and that healthy blood flow aids in prevention and facilitates healing, it follows that limiting blood flow will lead to degeneration. This is the same truth in our human physiology or for any animal. If the frog cannot make ground contact and function as it should, then shock cannot be properly absorbed, and blood cannot freely flow. When metal is nailed in all around, both proper blood circulation and shock absorption are dangerously impeded.

Along with back pain, foot pain is a common hotspot for problems in domestic horses. Again, it comes down to the differences between our domestic horses' lives and the lives of wild horses.

For the vast majority of horses' history as a species, all horses were barefoot. (Horses have been on the planet in the form of equus for 50 million years; people only started shoeing horses about 1,500 years ago.) Horses have been used for fieldwork, war, and performance in their natural barefoot state, even carrying fully armored men into battle.

Battle History—Why Shoes

The practice of shoeing horses began after soldiers started taking horses into battle. Soldiers wanted to have the horses they had trained, so a soldier would catch a horse from a natural environment, bring it into captivity, and train it.

In captivity, a few things happened. One is that the horse was no longer running and moving with the herd, foraging for food. This represented a radical change for animals meant to be constantly on the go. Limited motion meant that the blood-pumping mechanism of the hoof wasn't totally functioning. The resulting limited blood circulation translated to a significant lack of nutrient supply.

Secondly, because the horse was standing predominantly in a stall and often in his own excrement, the hoof became prone to infection and putrefied. So they thought, "How can we elevate the hoof out of the rot?"

At this point in history, people didn't understand the physiology of the hoof. They just knew they needed to protect their horses' hooves somehow, so they came up with the solution of nailing a solid metal plate onto the bottom of the hoof. That was the first hoof shoe. Also, stomping on the enemy with metal shoes made them fiercer war horses.

But alas, the rot worked its way between the metal plate and the hoof, making everything worse. Cutting out the middle of the plate was thought to allow the hoof to retain some breathability and air circulation. That's how the current horseshoe shape was developed.

Despite a millennium and a half of scientific advances, including the discovery of how a horse's hoof is meant to work, very little has changed since then in horseshoe design. We no longer take horses into battle, so the original purpose of metal shoes is no longer applicable. Yet, even with completely different conditions and all the knowledge we've gained, people still nail metal shoes to their horses' hooves—just as it's been done for the last 1,500 years. And if you think your horses need the protection of metal shoes, remember that the outside walls of the hoof are already hard. It's actually the softer, more vulnerable middle sole area that might welcome some protection.

If your horse seems distressed or isn't performing with freedom and ease, the problem can usually be traced to his back or feet. If you take steps to rule out these two potential problem areas, most horses will be more than 80% sound. These corrective measures are simple, but they may not be easy. The good news is that we no longer need to accept conventional views of lameness and disease as a required component of horse ownership. You can take comfort in the groundswell of trimmers and specialists emerging to assist you as you take responsibility for your horse's comfort and well-being.

"The blood in horses' feet does much more than provide nutrients to hoof tissues. It also enables the unshod foot to function as a hydraulic system, in much the same way that gel-filled athletic shoes do. We need to be trimming hooves so that more of the back part of the foot— including the frog—bears the initial ground impact forces and weight. Horseshoes provide a much smaller surface area to absorb shock. So if a bare hoof landing after a jump experiences, say, 1,000 pounds of loading per square foot, then with a traditional shoe, there's going to be 2,000 pounds per square foot."

– Dr. Robert Bowker, DVM- From Horse & Rider, Feb. 2006, "Is Barefoot Better?"

CAROLE HERDER

Natural Trimming

For your horse's best hoof health, it's essential to have a good trimmer. There are several differences between a good barefoot trim and the way hooves are trimmed to prepare them for metal shoes. It's important to find someone with experience in this area.

Many farriers are resisting the barefoot movement. It's sad because they've been the backbone of our industry for so many years. Some are set on keeping their old ways, but if they could just make the transition, they could retain their position as our primary source of hoof care. Helping horses go barefoot would take away the nailing metal in part of their responsibilities as a farrier, and some think therefore their livelihood. So of course they would want our horses to keep wearing metal shoes! If this is their position then, unfortunately, we can't really rely on them as the complete authority anymore. But I know several farriers who have progressed to barefoot hoof care. Their work is brilliant, and even though the job has changed, their income has not, and in some cases it has even increased.

Farrier Resistance

The truth is many of us have met with resistance, so we've taken it upon ourselves to study and train, and we've learned to trim our own horses' feet. As we started to have some success, our neighbors started asking us to trim their horses' feet, too. This vocation is now flourishing, and we horse owners are doing a job that was previously a masculine domain. It is a traditional trade that has advanced into a new craft and with it, a gender change. The barefoot movement is the most evolutionary development toward the health and well-being of our horses in history.

We now have enough evidence for change. We can look forward to a natural barefoot future for our horses—giving them freedom from the pain and problems most domestic horses experience—a future of greater health and better lives for years to come.

If you can't find anyone in your area that is trained as a natural trimmer, call Cavallo. We are here to help. I also recommend Liberated Horsemanship for training. They offer a great program where you can learn how to trim your own horses' hooves. You can find more information on that in the Resources section at the end of this book.

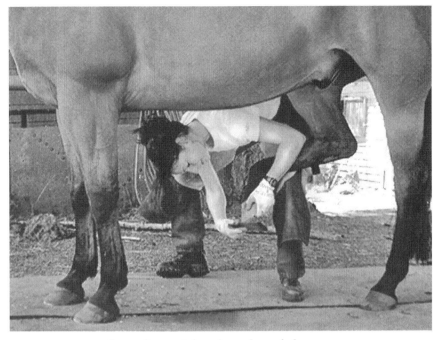

Lynn Spaan trimming a horse's hooves

100 Percent Barefoot?

With an excellent trimmer, can you pull off the shoes and immediately let your horse go barefoot like a wild horse?

In some cases, you can. If the horse's hooves are conditioned to the terrain with the extra weight of a rider, they can be 100 percent comfortable. For most of us, that is certainly not the case.

Why Can't My Horse Just Be Barefoot?

People have asked, "If metal shoes are so bad, why can't I just leave my horse barefoot?" Naturally, barefoot is nice for a number of reasons, such as increasing blood circulation, absorbing shock naturally, saving our terrain, preventing injuries between horses, allowing proper hoof mechanism and saving money; however, we must account for our horses' domestic condition.

CAROLE HERDER

Look at horses' hoof condition in relation to their living environment: grassy pastures and bedded stalls. They are conditioned to tolerate the terrain of their habitat. But then for 5 percent, or even a generous 10 percent of the time, we ask them to pack us up a gravelly trail or hard asphalt road. Their hoofs may not be accustomed to this terrain, and the load is increased with our weight and the weight of our saddles. This additional weight can be 20 percent of their own body weight, on average about 200 pounds. It presses the soles of their feet even further into the ground, and that's why they need the protection.

Most horses are uncomfortable travelling outside their living conditions with extra weight on bare feet. This makes the sole descend even further into that rough terrain, which the hooves are not conditioned to. It's clear that our horses do need protection in riding, but nailing metal shoes to their feet is not the answer. The shape of a metal shoe does nothing to protect their soles.

To see how this works, view this video from the Swedish Hoof School. Type the following link into your browser to view the video: https://goo.gl/oCO9ej

This is done with a cadaver and a hydraulic press. It starts by showing about 1,000 pounds—the average weight of a horse—coming down on this hoof. You can see the frog making contact with the ground, and you can see the heel spreading apart from side to side. You can also see how much blood is circulating in that area, and you can see the bone column descending.

The second half of the video shows what happens when you add additional pounds. If you watch, you can see how much more of that sole is compressed into the ground and how much wider those heels have to spread apart.

So, do our horses' hooves need protection when we're riding them? Yes, they do.

Hoof Boots

I use Cavallo hoof boots when riding. That's what I recommend as part of any successful barefoot program. They protect the hoof without interfering with its natural mechanism for shock absorption and blood flow, allowing you to go over any terrain at any speed. And unlike metal shoes, they provide all around hoof protection, especially for the soft part of the hoof. Hoof boots protect this area without interfering with the hoof's natural function. Take a metal shoe and bang it against a hard surface. You will feel the tremors vibrate up your arm. Try it. In fact, even the nails cause vibration which will compromise the integrity and break down hoof structure.

Before our current level of technology, metal may have been the best we could do, but now we have boots that absorb shock and provide protection on any terrain. Hoof boots absorb concussion rather than transmit it, so that the sensitive lamellae of the hoof are not compromised but instead are supported. The main support system of the coffin bone can remain strong and integral when the high-frequency vibration of impact on metal is not constantly jarring. Still don't think that it really matters? Try imagining going for a jog with metal shoes nailed to your feet. Ouch!

Healthy Feet

In 1984, Veterinary Medical Faculty Scientist, Luca Bein, the Swiss Cavalry at University of Zurich, Switzerland, conducted research into the effect of metal shoeing. Studies showed that the impact force a shod hoof receives on hard ground is 10 to 33 times that of an unshod hoof. The vibration in the hoof from the shoe is approximately 800 Hz. This level of vibration is high enough to destroy living tissue.

What's worse, metal horseshoes are nailed in all around, clamping the hoof in its smallest, most contracted position. The hoof can't spread, and the frog can't make ground contact. This doesn't just prevent the horse's natural shock absorption mechanism from working; it also dangerously impedes blood circulation.

We know that blood circulation is needed to distribute nutrients throughout the system and that healthy blood flow facilitates healing. If that blood flow is limited, it makes sense that the result will be degeneration.

CAROLE HERDER

Make a Heart Connection

The phrase "that horse is all heart" can mean that your horse cares about her connection with you. She wants to please you, serve you, and protect you. You can see the heart connection of horses in competition when they give their all. You've heard heroic stories of horses defying odds and instinct to flee in order to love, serve, and protect. You may find it interesting to note that Secretariat had the largest ever recorded heart at 12 pounds, while an average horse heart weighs seven to nine pounds.

We humans have a special place in our hearts for horses; they illicit warm yummy feelings for even those who aren't as lucky as you and me to be around horses.

This idea of the horse having five hearts—one in her chest and four on the ground—is three-fold. First, the heart is where love and emotion reside. Second, the heart is central to the health and life of any animal (or human). Third, as in any animal, the horse's heart pumps blood to circulate through the body, providing oxygen and nutrients to the body's cells, organs, and structure, which includes the feet.

Different from other animals, the structure and function of the frogs of a horse's hooves are just as critical to the circulatory system as the heart. Each time the hoof makes contact with the ground it expands and pumps blood like the heart. Blood is life. That function is arrested when metal shoes are used and is ultimately harmful to your horse. This is my *"why."* This is the reason I produce and promote the use of hoof boots.

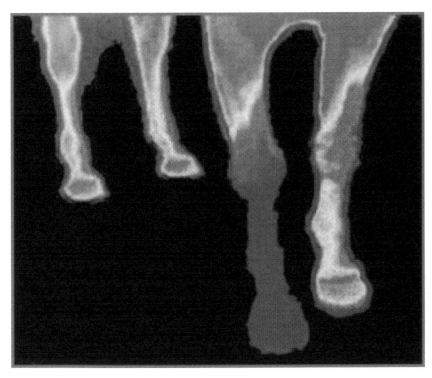

Which hoof do you think has a metal shoe nailed on? It's the darker one in the foreground—you can tell because the blood isn't circulating. I remember when I first got into horses, I was told that you feel down the legs and when you get to the knee, it starts to cool off, and when you get to the hoof, it should feel nice and cool.

Nice and cool? How can it be nice and cool if blood is circulating?

I'm not saying a hoof should be hot. It shouldn't—a hot hoof would indicate inflammation. But it should be warm. You should be able to feel blood circulation.

Remember, horses have five hearts, so those frogs function to pump the blood through all the coriums of the hoof and then back up to the heart. That's the natural wild horse way, and you should feel warmth in your horse's legs, too.

Here's what one vet, Dr. Thomas Teskey, had to say about the effects of metal shoes:

"Every horse that wears steel shoes suffers some degree of laminar separation. There are a myriad of other malfunctions that also occur in a shod hoof, and they all contribute to the hoof functioning in a completely different and abnormal fashion and it leads to a severe contraction in their size, so much so that when the shoe is removed the horses can no longer walk comfortably on their own feet.

"For the presence of steel on a horse's feet, we are able to observe profound damages that occur due to the stagnation of blood within the hoof and the diminished return of blood back up toward the heart through the veins of the lower leg. Metal shoes interfere with the hoof's natural blood-pumping mechanism. Period.

"I will never ask any client of mine to consider shoeing their horse with steel. I have conviction in my belief about this, and it is unwavering. I feel that farriers and veterinarians and trainers and horse people must learn the truth about this and tell their clients, friends, and colleagues that shoeing horses damages them and robs them of years of their lives."

—*Dr. Tomas Teskey, DVM*

Navicular Disease

Metal horseshoes are nailed on when the horse's hoof is in the air, at its smallest, most contracted shape. The hoof is not expanded with weight bearing or movement, and the metal nailed onto it holds it in this shape, preventing the heel from spreading when the horse's weight is on the hoof. Since the heel can't spread under weight, the frogs can't pump blood through all the coriums of the hoof and back up through the legs to the heart. In effect, metal shoes prevent the blood circulation that would provide the very nutrients needed to prevent or alleviate many of the conditions our horses are plagued with.

Also, since the heel can't spread, the coffin bone can't drop like a trampoline as the weight of the horse comes down. But there's still 1,000 pounds of horse coming down on a little hoof, and it's got to go somewhere.

With the natural shock-absorption mechanism immobilized, where is the shock absorbed? Perhaps it's absorbed in the sensitive tissue of the hoof or further up the structure of the leg.

As the coffin bone pushes down under the horse's weight, it may bruise the solar corium because the sole can't draw flat to get out of the way. The pain caused as a result of a bruised solar corium is often sadly misdiagnosed as "navicular syndrome." We must ask, "Is it the pressure from the descending coffin bone, or is it the damaged bone that is painful?"

Under radiographs, the bone is often shown to be deteriorating. Enlarged holes and passageways through the bone are a result of congested blood. Lack of circulation causes the arteries to swell, pushing against the bone. This causes deterioration to bone spongiosa. The real cause of bone corrosion is often the lack of blood circulation. Additional pain results through irritation of connective tissue, stress on ligaments and tendons, and bruising when bone tissue meets corium.

We call the vet because our horse is lame, and too often the horse is diagnosed as "navicular." However, instead of treating the cause by re-establishing natural hoof function, we treat the symptoms. We have bar shoes applied, and the horse walks off, supposedly sound. We think the bar shoes are an extraordinary cure, when what is really happening may be just the opposite—even less circulation!

In a normal horseshoe shape, the frog still makes some contact with the ground and pumps blood at that spot. With a bar across the heel, circulation is completely inhibited.

The horse can walk only because he can't feel his feet. His hoof is numb, while the internal damage continues. Pain medication can also mask the condition. The proliferation and growing use of products containing glucosamine, MSM, and anti-inflammatories is a result of our inadequate understanding of the shock- absorbing features of the hoof.

The only real cure is to treat the cause of the problems, not the symptoms. Allowing our horses' hooves to function more naturally will decrease their pain and discomfort. This means pulling off the metal shoes and rehabilitating the hoof to perform its natural function.

The upside of all this is that not only does this allow your horse a more holistic healthy lifestyle but you gain the opportunity of a better and deeper connection.

DR. ROBERT COOK:

"All horses' hooves are healthier without shoes, and barefoot horses are healthier than shod horses. They live longer, happier, less painful lives. Barefoot is a requirement for health and should be accepted as a condition for keeping a horse. Humane management is not just preferable, it is non-negotiable.

The foot evolved to function unshod. Nature has developed the perfect design for grip and slide in all conditions and provided for unsurpassable shock absorption. The foot cannot expand and contract with each step when clamped. Blood supply to the foot is impoverished and horn production becomes deficient. When the foot is prevented from functioning correctly, the pastern, fetlock, cannon, and knee are also placed at risk. This leads to bone, joint, & soft tissue injuries."

- Dr. Robert Cook, FRCVS, PhD, Professor of Surgery Emeritus at Tufts University

19

HORSES ARE IN NOW

We live in a world that is in constant motion with a hustle mentality, lamenting the past either consciously or unconsciously. The imprints left on the subconscious mind by past experience colour all of life, one's nature, responses, states of mind, planning, and betting on the future. So much of our energy and effort is put into doing something to get something else down the road hoping that our future is better than our present, or in some cases so that we can recreate a past we wish we had never lost. We humans get tangled up in time along with the emotions and expectations of the past and future, so much so that we ignore the present. We can avoid this illusionary sense of what is by self-exploration to the physical sensations of our body that continuously interconnect with the conditions of our mind. It is a journey to free us from living our lives as a result of things we remember or anticipation of things we desire. In contrast, our horses are different. They simply live in the now.

The evolutionary state of your horse is just *to be*. He's not caught up in thinking, feeling, and doing. His state of being is so beautiful and full of possibilities. He's not hung up on relationship issues, bad things that have happened, or sadness. Nor is he scheduled for every second of the next three weeks, positioning his life around a to-do list. That's our unfortunate evolutionary state—busy with our focus on the past or future instead of the present. You may have constant thoughts, worries, a list of "honey do's" floating around in your head, but your horse doesn't. He is there, with you, in that moment, completely. Doesn't he deserve the same presence from you? Just to be there.

I don't want to imply that horses live in a state of amnesia with no connection to their past. They are aware of what they have learned in the past, but only as it relates to what is happening in the present so that they can act appropriately to their current environment. Let me give you an example. My horse, Slash, is somewhat afraid of dogs because he was attacked by a pack of dogs as a young colt. When the dogs approached him, instinctually, he ran. Of course, he outran the dogs, but in his haste to get away he ran into a tree and was injured to the point that he has a big scar because of it. It looks like he was slashed by a knife not a tree branch, hence his name "Slash." He's not afraid of trees, though; he's afraid of dogs. So when we encounter a dog out on a trail, he is a bit wary.

Now he doesn't stand around all day preoccupied about dogs thinking, "Oh man, I remember when that dog incident happened, and it really freaks me out." He doesn't ruminate on the past. When he sees a dog he is cautious and a little edgy, but it doesn't affect his persona ongoing. He will respond to a dog in the moment, but the bad experience of the past doesn't change his entire personality day in and day out like the past can shape and fully change the emotional and mental well-being of people. If a horse is abused it isn't a memory he reflects on, it is a learning that he had from an experience that he draws upon when similar situations arise in his life that cause him to be afraid. When we get a horse, and we don't know his history, you can't assume his behavior is because he is bad, but that it may be a response to a trigger. You can't hold that against him. Be patient while being safe and recondition your horse to connect a new, safe experience with that trigger.

I know this concept of learning without direct memory seems odd to us. Think of it like this. When you have kids, you can tell them not to touch the hot stove because it will burn. Inevitably, your daughter will either purposefully or by accident touch the stove and get burnt. She isn't destined to grow up with a fear of stoves and a sharp memory of when she got burnt, but the experience will impact her future behavior around stoves. It is the same type of behavioral learning for your horse. Just as much as your horse doesn't bemoan the past, he doesn't worry about the future either. When I take Slash on a trail ride, he isn't thinking, "Gosh, I hope we don't run into those dogs." He thinks about it right when we come to where the dogs are. Right as we come around that bend. Not when we head out the driveway. Imagine if he did. Oh yeah, you can imagine it because you've likely experienced it worrying about something in a future that hasn't happened yet and is not likely to happen. We humans all do it, but what a waste of time and energy.

Many preoccupations are about fears that do not ever materialize. We humans can be immobilized by our fears when we constantly project into the future. We also miss the joys of the present because we're busy evaluating the past or are focused on the future. The present moment is where happiness is, where creativity and true understanding lie. The present moment is where God exists, where we exist. Whatever your religious or spiritual beliefs are, they can only be experienced in present time.

More On Presence

I have referenced the importance of being present with your horse throughout this book. I shared my ritual of walking in the barn, taking a deep breath and releasing whatever I don't need to take in with me. I leave my troubles, frustrations, and pre- occupations at the door. I want to and need to be present with my horse. I want to stay in the present moment so that I can fully enjoy the friendship, beauty and pleasure of this magnificent creature. I want to be able to soak up every bit of our time, training, and riding together through my body and all my senses. I don't just want to do something with my horse; I want to *be* with my horse. If I let all the chatter in my head from the rest of my day of emotions carry over, it will dull my senses and preoccupy me from making the most of the present moment.

I am quite certain you have the same desire to fully experience interactions with your horse, and I am quite certain that you get distracted by the buzzing of thoughts and the power of emotions. If you can learn to release all of it and be in the present with your horse, the joy will be exponential. Don't get me wrong. I am not saying I can do that all the time. It's just that I try not to be duped to follow the thread of the 60,000 mostly irrelevant thoughts that I have every day. And every now and again, I am there, right in the moment with no thoughts luring me away from the beauty of my horse, the beauty of life.

You read about intuition at other points in this book. The best way to fully enjoy your horse and care for him—well actually, the best way to fully enjoy and care for your own life—is to live through your heart, senses, and intuition and let them inform your mind. How? You accomplish this by being present. The more you are able to be present and approach life through your heart and intuition the more you'll start to trust your internal knowing over anything external—anything "scientifically" proven, which can change. Anything anyone tells you. It is this inner knowing, your fine-tuned intuition, that can lead you to question the status quo.

The more present and intuitively we live the less we accept things without feeling they're true and right. If your gut tells you something is wrong, then it is an opportunity to creatively make a different choice. When you hear the truth, you really know it. That's how so much innovation is sparked, by looking for a better way. Maybe the guy who cut you off in traffic just lost his job and has a bleeding ulcer and an addicted teenager. It's not our fault, but he is just so lost, he's flipping everyone the finger that day. Don't take it personally. Move on.

When I got quieter within and started to question things that were generally accepted, I started to feel good. And that's what I want. I want to feel good. That's how I came to seek out and create hoof boots. I didn't feel good about having metal nailed into my horse's feet, even though most everyone else was doing it. I trusted my intuition to embrace something that made me feel good and discard that which did not.

Circulate Love

There is a universal law of relationships which states "what you reap, so shall you sow every day of your life." You get what you put in. It's an energetic force of nature, circulating and flowing like blood. Give what you want to get. If you want a kind and joyful relationship, that is what you must put forward. Horses are extremely sensitive to their surroundings, so when you allow good energy to circulate, they pick up on it right away. When you activate certain attitudes like love, compassion, gentleness, joy, equanimity, and self-awareness, your horse responds in kind. If you have children, you know you must love unconditionally but also take the lead. Taking the lead, we must make choices that do not reinforce any patterns other than an understanding that we always receive a version of what we offer.

Trainer and clinician, Julie Goodnight, is a beautiful example of this as she endeavors to assist us with our horse training to display leadership and provide safety and assurance to our horses. Once this is implicit, we can better establish relationship and direction. It's a clear and consistent method. We are the trusted authority.

We talked earlier about limbic resonance, or limbic regulation, being the contagion of mood and emotions. Certainly, the higher frequencies transmit readily, but so do the lower ones. We actually match each other's energy. Have you ever noticed a conversation where someone appears to be in a negative state? "Oh, I am so sick, my head aches, and I'm coughing," which is met with comments like, "That's nothing, I was throwing up, I was so sick."

It is unfortunate but seemingly much more often that these negative energies are passed from one to the other. It's amazing really. Molecules exchange—we breathe in molecules, and we breathe out molecules. So in a very straightforward way, you are inhaling your horse's breath, and your horse is inhaling yours. You are exchanging carbon dioxide and oxygen that comes from your cells with those of your horse. They are real and measureable molecules, so in a very real sense when we are together with our horses we are really together in more tangible ways than we may think.

Bad Horse

This may all sound too idealistic. So what if you have a really "bad" horse? He rears, bucks, and runs off, and you are afraid of him. Start at the ground and work your way through. Do not do anything that scares you. Just realize that he is not a static being destined to remain that way forever. Everything is changing, and you absolutely influence which direction it goes. Every little thing you do becomes the sum of the whole. You can't cheat. Horses are way too smart for that. You have to cope with integrity in every event; you must be honest or your horse will call you out and won't trust you next time. Sometimes you just don't have the time and patience, and that's OK, too. Just realize that you've got your set of circumstances that you came to the relationship with, and so does your horse. The respective baggage may just be something that isn't ready to move yet. Don't force the issue. Try your best. Be kind. Be gentle. Try more subtlety. Be responsible for what you bring into his space. Give more.

And if you just can't get along with your horse, do both of you a favor and move on. It happens. Many think they want horses, but then somehow it's just not quite right. Or they think they want to show jump or barrel race, and they get this really flashy high- performance horse and they think,

"Oh, something is really wrong with this horse" when really if they look honestly in the mirror they might find a mountain trail rider is more their style. I've had friends who wanted to marry a cowboy or a football player and then when it comes right down to it that isn't the truth for them at all. They liked the illusion, not the truth. They liked the picture and then created a story around it, and that's all it was—a story. You don't have to be anything for anyone. Just be true to yourself; the answers will come when the time is perfect.

What about mistakes? We all make them. Sometimes we know we're making them at the time but the choice meets our need in the moment. Sometimes we don't have all the facts or make assumptions, and it turns out we were wrong. Sometimes we had all the best intentions, and the results created unintended consequences, or it just didn't work out. It is what it is. Own it and move forward. What matters is that you learn from it, make a change in course or choose differently next time. I can't lament about the choices in feed, metal shoes, and other care I used to make for my horses. What matters is that I acknowledged what I knew in my heart, listened to my horse and made better choices going forward. What is just as important is to appreciate what is going right. Perhaps you made a choice to jump a few 3.5 hurdles, and it didn't quite work out as you were hoping; your horse wasn't quite ready. Every choice that doesn't work out isn't dire. It is just a learning experience. You can still enjoy the next ride.

The Karma of Choices

Choices have consequences, good and bad, expected and unintentional. The outcomes of your choices may not be evident today or even next year. However, know that who you are now is a result of the choices you made five years ago, three months ago and yesterday. So the choices you're making today will create your tomorrow, your year and your ten years from now.

Dr. Michelle Robin, author of *The E Factor: Engage, Energize, Enrich – Three Steps to Vibrant Health,* talks a lot about the com- pounding effects of the small decisions we make. She refers to them as debits and credits to your health account. Building health is not unlike building wealth. It is the compounded effects of the little choices (and some big choices) that create your future in every aspect of your life. Some of those little choices are preventative measures. You brush your teeth for good breath, a white smile and to keep your teeth. You take your car in for oil changes, a fluid check and tire rotation to keep it running well and lasting longer. One of my good friends tells me that I live a high-octane life, so I'd better put premium fuel in. I am travelling a lot and speaking and presenting and running a business and being a mother and a wife and trying to learn to be a better person, so I fuel myself with good supplements, receive acupuncture or massage, exercise and meditate. To me, this is the quality of the fuel required to live this full life.

You keep your horse's hooves trimmed and hydrated. You make sure he is fed all day, has his coat brushed, is exercised and socialized, and you do other preventative and maintenance efforts to stave off issues and create a foundation for a healthy and happy horse. The difficult thing about making the good choices that build health (and wealth) is that we often don't feel or see results right away. We want it now. It is enjoyable now to spend five dollars a day on a Starbucks cappuccino versus putting an extra $150 a month towards savings. It is more fun to watch another sitcom than take those thirty minutes five days a week to exercise. I read once, "Don't do what you want, and you may do what you like." See, if you eat the cake and burgers now because you want to, you may eventually not be able to go on those walks through the forest that you like. If you want to order a second bottle of wine with dinner, you may find yourself lying in bed with a headache and an Advil in the morning, and you don't like to take pharmaceuticals, but you do like to go for a morning run.

We live in a Western society that in recent decades has shifted far more toward a culture of instant gratification. It causes us to want to satiate our desires right now, often not thinking about the long-term impact for ourselves, others, or the world. I dare say it is partially the root of why our nations are in such heavy debt, why so many adults and now children are obese, why our environment is struggling, and so on. When making choices in your life—be they about health, food, career, treatment of others, etc.—consider both the short-term and long-term consequences for yourself and others. Know that the choices you make and their results are yours alone to own and reject.

The first and most ancient language, Sanskrit, has a word called karma that refers to the concept that every action has an equal and opposite reaction. It means voluntary as well as unconscious acts lead to the fruits or consequences that arise from these acts. Some people console themselves that if people are bad or cruel that karma will get them. This may or may not happen, because it is about thought patterns, too. You can create what you think about. You get what you give. Our karma, the consequences of the choices we make, can deliver love and light or a daily prison of fear and loneliness. If we continue to make the same poor choices every day and don't see the big picture, we might miss the open door to fulfillment that we could have walked through. We go for the quick win, the instant satisfaction, the convenience. Unless your decisions bring you love, joy, and well-being, then you are in a trap and need to make different choices. A popular phrase now is that the definition of insanity is taking the same action and expecting a different result. I encourage you to examine the life you have built, the body and health you've created and question if you feel love, joy and well-being, your human rights.

Are the choices you're making for your horse helping to generate a life of love, joy, and well-being for him? He will show you how he feels, the results of the actions taken or not taken in the past. It is our job to listen, look, and then question the choices being made that are creating our horse's state of well-being. I was indoctrinated into the horse world with the idea that you nail metal shoes on hooves. I struggled with the idea from the beginning and was met with the comment that maybe I shouldn't have horses if I can't even accept that. After all, it has been a practice for 1,500 years.

When I started questioning it because it weighed heavy on my heart, I was ridiculed and shunned. I had to follow my heart and make a different choice for my horse and myself. The external short-term consequences were difficult, caused by the reaction of others and feeling very alone. This was indeed several years ago, and support was limited. Often the day-to-day feeling was a struggle, but looking to the long-term I felt light in my heart. The long-term external consequences have been great as I have been able to create hoof boots for my horses and hundreds of thousands of other horses. My horses are healthier and happier, and I get to share my passions with other horse lovers around the world.

20

COMPETITIVE EDGE

We care about our horses in a way that mimics our natural nurturing instincts. For some of us, horses incite more compassion than even human family members. We want to make sure we're doing what's best for our horses and giving them everything they need to live happy, healthy lives.

Throughout this book, I've shared the things I've learned so that you can use this knowledge to provide better lives for your horses.

You may remember that I previously talked about my sweet beauty, *AsBadAsMyDad—my Dot.* When she started having the same problems Rocky had, I knew I had to do something to keep her from suffering the same fate he did.

And so does this story have a happy ending? Yes, it does.

Dot and I started training for my sport of barrel racing, and she got it immediately. But the consistency didn't emerge. Some days she was fine and others she was stiff, swollen, and crabby. I went down every path imaginable trying to determine the problem, from traditional radiographs to alternative body work—all inconclusive. You know the story: navicular, ring bone, splints, bar shoes at age 9 and "Buted" with pads by 14. I could not accept it and had to find the answer. And then I realized with astonishing certainty that her problem came from the feet.

Now that my horses are barefoot, they are all happy and healthy. I no longer have to accept that 12 is old age for a horse. Dot has now joined me in the finest time this cowgirl could ever imagine. We shaved 1.2 seconds off our best time in barrel racing, and it's because she was barefoot. She was able to run flat out, without the hard concussion and the 800-hertz frequency that would be reverberating back up her structure if she were wearing metal shoes. Her hooves could absorb shock properly, and she had plenty of traction. Remember, this horse was bred to compete, and pain free she does it magnificently.

Rehabilitating her to be comfortable barefoot was a challenge at first. I would be hand walking her up and down the roads with my friends saying I was crazy. "Put some shoes on, come and ride!" But I just knew I would never nail another metal shoe on a horse again. Discovering hoof boots made the whole process easy. And the next spring we were back on the circuit—barefoot!

It was a bit funny to return to barrel racing. The girls welcomed me back, then realizing Dot was barefoot and thinking I had fallen on hard times, they offered to lend me money to shoe my horse. I politely declined. They were all fairly surprised at her increased competitive edge and the performance of her naturally bare hooves. You can imagine the interest back then when Dot ran with full hoof function: coffin bone dropping like a trampoline to absorb shock, hoof mechanism operating to increase traction. No pain. No restriction. Running flat out and around those barrels in three rather than four strides, shaving over a second off our time.

Go Dot!

Since we've been on a successful barefoot program, we haven't had any problems with lameness or injuries. My Slash is 27 years old, and he runs around like a 5-year-old in bare feet. If you had told me 20 years ago that a love of horses and discovering barrel racing would develop my character and chart a course to life—altering my path in everything I do—I would have said, no way. Through this experience, I not only saved my own horses but also developed a company that is committed to saving the lives of horses all over the world. I have realized that I can create myself and my life the way I want them to be.

So Thankful For Rocky

All that I have today was made possible because of Rocky. It's because of his problems that I became passionate in my efforts to make him more comfortable. I immersed myself in research and study. What I learned as a result has helped to change the lives of other horses for the better.

Rocky also left me with a love for speed and barrel racing, which I still have today. I will always be grateful to him for forging a new path, breaking new ground and encouraging me out of necessity to think differently, changing my life and the lives of hundreds of thousands of horses around the world forever.

Cavallo Hoof Boots—over any terrain at any speed

CAROLE HERDER

It was never my expectation that horse hooves would become my passion and purpose. Some people are fortunate to know what they want at an early age, and they simply follow their path to attain it. I, on the other hand, began with quite a different kind of picture for my life. The transformation was somewhat of an expansion period, fraught with growing pains that were at times so severe I wanted to turn and run back to the old life I knew. At times I felt like I should stop trying to blaze a trail to the unfamiliar, the unprecedented. My dear Oma left me with the prophesy that helped to overcome those dark times when she said, "Your purpose in life is preordained. Don't ever doubt yourself." We are all here to express our authentic selves. The task is in discovering who that is.

FREE BONUSES!

Send an email to Bonuses@CaroleHerder.com, and you will receive immediate and exclusive access to these great interviews and webinars:

HOOF HEALTH: FACT VS FICTION

Dr. Tomas Teskey explains his purpose of Veterinary Oath and his theories on natural hoof care. Gain a better understanding of hoof function through his easy-going nature and clear, concise delivery, supported by graphic illustrations.

WHY HORSES CAN'T GO BAREFOOT

Dr. Tomas Teskey delivers an in-depth look at overall horse physiology. Learn horse care requirements from a physical and psychological standpoint, including dentistry and its effect on hoofs.

CAROLE'S "FIRESIDE CHAT" WITH MONTY ROBERTS

Monty's 80 years on the planet embraces extensive travel, interesting relationships and unwavering commitment to improve the lives of horses and humans. This webinar will leave you uplifted and inspired.

Just send an email to Bonuses@CaroleHerder.com to receive instant access!

ABOUT THE AUTHOR

Carole Herder has a genuine passion for educating horse owners worldwide, especially on all matters related to natural horse keeping. Carole gives presentations and leads workshops at horse events worldwide.

Carole's involvement in the study of horse health began in 1994, as a result of insurmountable health problems experienced by her beloved first horse, Rocky. It was her love for Rocky that spurred her to learn all she could about horse health, and eventually to found Cavallo Horse & Rider, Inc. She went on to design the Total Comfort System Saddle Pads; Cavallo Simple, Sport, ELB, Transporter and Trek Hoof Boots.

Carole is a certified Chopra University Instructor. In 2010, she won the Royal Bank of Canada western division Trail Blazer Woman Entrepreneur

CAROLE HERDER

of the year award. Her work is changing the world and blazing a new trail in an otherwise stagnant, traditional industry. Carole is a proud member of the WPO—Women Presidents Organization, supporting women in business.

Through her work and designs, she has served hundreds of thousands of horses and riders around the world. Providing comfort for horses is her goal. You can contact Carole at:

info@cavallo-inc.com or toll free at 1-877-818-0037,

or through her website: www.cavallo-inc.com.

RESOURCES

Throughout this book I have shared several quotes from those who have provided inspiration to give me strength in this journey. The following are listed here for you:

Alice Walker

http://womenshistory.about.com/od/alicewalker/a/alice_walker.htm

Carl Sagan   http://www.carlsagan.com/

Dr Wayne Dyer   http://www.drwaynedyer.com/

Marianne Williamson   http://marianne.com/

Pam Brown

www.poetryinternationalweb.net/pi/site/poet/item/685

Robert   Oppenheimer   http://www.famousscientists.org/j-robert-oppenheimer/

This is an amazing book about the idea of limbic resonance:

http://www.amazon.ca/General-Theory-Love-Thomas-Lewis/dp/0375709223

This book can help support your health goals:

http://www.drmichellerobin.com/product/e-factor/

Here is a video link to the Jill Bolte Taylor presentation documenting her own stroke:

https://www.ted.com/talks/jill_bolte_taylor_s_powerful_stroke_of_insight?language=en

A good resource to learn about trimming methods:

http://www.liberatedhorsemanship.com/Liberated_Horsemanship_Home.html

http://strasserhoofcare.org/

Here you can learn about Paddock Paradise:

http://www.jaimejackson.com/

The Stories from my friends and a very short list of some of my favorite people:

Monty Roberts http://www.montyroberts.com/

Julie Goodnight http://juliegoodnight.com/

Pat & Linda Parelli http://www.parelli.com/

Dan James & Dan Steers

http://www.doubledanhorsemanship.com/

Guy McLean http://www.guymcleanusatour.com/

Joe Camp http://thesoulofahorse.com/

Dr. Deepak Chopra https://www.deepakchopra.com/

DVM Tomas Teskey

http://www.equinesciencesacademy.com/esa_000026.htm

Learn everything you need to know about saddle pads:

https://www.cavallo-inc.com/saddle-pad-technology/

The individual Veterinarians who were quoted are as follows:

Robert Bowker, VMD, Ph.D

http://www.equinesciencesacademy.com/esa_000070.htm

Dr. Tomas G. Teskey

http://www.equinesciencesacademy.com/esa_000026.htm

Dr. Robert Cook, FRCVS., PhD.

http://www.bitlessbridle.com/index.php?main_page=page&id=5

A resource for horse keeping and the video clip on hoof blood circulation:

http://swedishhoofschool.com/

https://goo.gl/oCO9ej

American Competitive United Kingdom TREC   Best of America   Australian Trail Horse   Liberated
Trail Horse Association   by Horseback   Riders Association   Horsemanship

WHAT OTHERS ARE SAYING ABOUT CAVALLO

"I want to thank Cavallo for such a wonderful hoof boot. I want to let you know that when I got my sweet Bella four years ago she came to me with already damaged hooves on her front. One was so bad she abscessed from every possible location, and just when we thought it was over it would erupt again. She was lame for an entire year while she grew a new hoof. Honestly, I did not think I would ever be able to ride her again and used to just spend as much time with her as I could talking to her and caring for her, but deep in my heart I was crying, not knowing what was going to happen. The thought of never riding with her again was devastating.

"She has since healed. I went over shoes in depth with my wonderful farrier and vet (knowing it was not what I wanted for her)—the thought of nailing metal on her already aching feet made me cringe. I could not imagine how in the world that could improve her feet. I spoke with them about boots, and we all agreed metal was not the route. I started searching and found Cavallo and ordered a pair of hoof boots. That was three years ago. I was nervous at first, thinking she would not be able to canter with them, but with time and the pastern wraps, she has taken to them perfectly, and we gallop full speed ahead through the grassy fields and go all day through rocky terrain on the trails, through mud, and swim in the water.

"She is so happy; my girl loves to run in the wind. She is my best friend, and I would do anything for her. Of course, when Cavallo came out with the color purple, I had to buy them as that is her color! She picks her feet right up for her boots; she knows she is going to have fun! We love our boots, and I have five other horses and will surely be 'booting' up any who are sensitive."

– Rose, USA

∞

"I started trimming this mare on September 6, 2010. Her name is Lilla Gumman (Swedish for "Little Darling"). She is a 14-year-old Kentucky Mountain saddle horse. She foundered badly around the end of May 2010 after her blacksmith told her owner to put her on straight alfalfa as she was losing weight. She was on sweet feed as well. She had been laying down most of the time for four months prior to me seeing her. The vet had said to keep her in a small stall in deep sand. Within two days she developed terrible sores all over her body from lying in the sand. Her owner, Margarhetta, put her in a larger stall with deep shavings and the mare did not develop any more sores, but she was still laying down most of the time. Margarhetta's friend told her about me and that I was an accomplished barefoot trimmer with experience with foundered horses.

"The veterinarian met me there and took X-rays of all four feet. She had foundered on all four, but the back feet were the worst. The right hind had a 25-degree rotation, and the left hind was a horrible 30-degree rotation with imminent coffin bone penetration. You could put a ruler on p1-2 and 3 and draw a straight line down all the bones to the bottom of the hoof, that is how severe the rotation was in the left hind. The mare was very bony, and her eyes were dull and lackluster. She had horizontal lines across her abdomen from the pain. This brave, wonderful mare wanted badly to live and wouldn't give up. She helped me all she could to stand and give me her feet, even if it was only for a few seconds at a time. Thank goodness for power tools, the grinder was amazing for working on foundered feet where the poor horse can't hold the feet up for very long. Sometimes you only get a few seconds.

"After her trim I immediately put her back feet in the Cavallo Simple Boots. We cut out rubber pads for her, and I instructed Margarhetta to leave her stall door open so she could have 24-hour access to her large pasture. The mare went right out and walked into the pasture for the first time in months. I then made her custom rubber/silicone pads. The mare

192

progressively walked more and more, laying down less and less. All with no Bute or medications! She wore the Cavallo hoof boots 24/7 for three months while she grew enough sole under the toe of the coffin bone. She rarely lies down now, has put her weight back on, and has the joy of life back in her eyes.

"Her diet was the second thing I changed after doing the first trim. We put her on molasses-free beet pulp, sunflower seeds, whole flaxseed, probiotics, and tested low sugar timothy hay. She has not suffered another laminitic attack since I started with her. Margarhetta has been so diligent in following all my instructions. She cleans the feet daily, does the white lightning soaks to keep them disease free and puts socks on her feet before she puts them in the Cavallo hoof boots, which really helps to prevent chafing as she was in the boots for so long. She loves this mare and is thrilled that Lilla Gumman is going to make a full recovery.

"Margarhetta is now taking her on long walks, and the mare marches right alongside her, totally pain free. I was thrilled by how the Cavallo hoof boots stayed on the feet and gave the mare the ability to walk while her feet healed. They were easy for Margarhetta to take on and off and did not torque the hoof in any way, no pressure pulling or yanking with these boots! They gave her stability and comfort while she healed. Today, after three months, we finally took them off and the mare walked out to her pasture comfortably.

"Thank you, Cavallo!" - Marianne Allen (Know Hoof, Know Horse Barefoot Practitioner)

WHAT OTHERS ARE SAYING ABOUT CAVALLO

UPDATE:

"I have an update for you on Lilla Gumman. On January 10, I spoke with Margaretta. She was so excited she could hardly contain herself! Lilla Gumman was cantering, trotting, and gaiting beautifully in her pasture for the first time since she had foundered last year. I had started trimming her September 6, so in just a little over four months of correct trimming this mare has made a complete recovery from a devastating founder! I actually cried when she told me how beautiful Lilla was moving, pain-free and a joyful horse once again! It is a very emotional experience to see a horse that was in such pain recover and regain her health.

"The Cavallo boots were an integral part of the healing process and were a big factor in keeping the mare moving and comfortable during her rehabilitation. This sped up the healing process considerably! Movement, movement, movement is the key to their healing, and if they are comfortable enough to walk, they will do so and heal. Thank you for being so proactive and innovative in your boot design, as they have helped out many horses I have worked on become sound again."

- Marianne Allen

∞

"I have the boots, and we put ice studs in them. I have a Rocky Mountain horse, and I'm happy to report we gait through the snow and ice as if it were summertime. We love riding in winter. Thanks to Cavallo boots, with ice studs added, our barefoot horses can move safely in the snow. Thank you for the great product!" - Gerda

∞

"Cavallo Sport boots did not come off! Tuesday (August 12, 2014) I went on a trail ride with my Rocky Mountain horse, Harley, wearing his front Cavallo Sport boots, which had 20+ miles on them at this point. We had received three to four inches of rain in the three days prior, so the terrain was VERY muddy. We crossed many muddy areas where they sank almost to their knees. At the worst point of the ride, we encountered a large tree that completely blocked the trail. The only way we could find to get around without turning around and backtracking for a couple of hours was to dismount and walk the horses through a soft grassy area into a rhododendron patch and back across another soft grassy area. My horse, Harley, and I went through first.

Unfortunately, the grassy areas turned out to be muddy bogs. In the first area, Harley sunk up to his knees. The second area Harley sunk in almost to his belly. Thankfully, he managed to get through on his own. And amazingly his Cavallo boots stayed on! In fact, his boots stayed on the entire ride. There was only one time I dismounted to refasten the strap on each boot that had come undone after crossing mud. I wanted you to know how well these boots have been working in very difficult situations."

- Debbie

ଚ

"I imagine that my comments may come off like some kind of shameless endorsement, but I have to thank you for your Cavallo Simple Boot design.

"We're located in the high desert 'Great Basin' region of Nevada. A typical ride in these parts may involve riding over prehistoric lake bed sand to footing that resembles cobblestone streets to picking our way through lava rock. All of our horses are barefoot. Barefoot horses seem to have healthier feet, and they get better traction on tricky terrain. However, a few of the horses need additional protection when traveling the rougher routes.

"We've accumulated various makes and models of equine boots over the years, but the Simple Boot is what we now reach for. We can put them on quickly and reliably without having to have a toolbox handy. The Velcro design is strong but also allows easy adjustment so that the boots will fit properly.

"They provide hoof wall protection without producing sores along the coronet or heel bulbs. Plus, these boots are really good at resisting sand intrusion when going through the really fluffy stuff, and surprisingly, the Velcro does not collect foxtails, burrs and the like.

"If we do trek across our own version of the Sahara Desert, it only takes a few seconds to remove a Simple Boot to check for sand (usually not a problem) and clean out the boot if a little sand did sneak in.

"To be honest, the Simple Boot actually changed my attitude about equestrian boots. Not that I didn't recognize their value, but I dreaded struggling with getting boots fitted properly before the ride, getting my fingers pinched in the mechanisms, cutting a finger on a frayed wire, or having to pull out a set of pliers to get the latches set to a proper tension—not to mention dealing with sand-caused sores on the horses after riding through really deep stuff.

"I obviously recommend equine boots for horses that need hoof protection, but I would advise anyone like me who has struggled with the older boot designs to look into the newer designs and technologies before giving up on the concept. Designs such as I found with Simple Boots can be game changers.

"If you decide to use my comments as a testimonial, I'd like to clarify that while I've always advocated for proper hoof care, this note about Simple Boots was completely unsolicited. I simply like equestrians to be aware of their options in order to make their experiences safer and more enjoyable for them and their mounts. Plus, we equestrians tend to be traditional, and we sometimes aren't aware of useful improvements in available horse equipment.

"So props to Cavallo for coming up with the Simple Boot. We've now used them long enough to be confident in their functionality and durability. And please continue to develop newer and better ways to protect our equine partners. Equestrian 'engineering' is a never-ending evolutionary process."

Warmest regards,

- Willis Lamm LRTC Wild Horse Mentors LRTC Large Animal Rescue Team

৪১

"I recently purchased two pairs of Simple Boots, and I am very satisfied. They are simply a dream to put on and fit really well. My horse has white hooves that easily crack on the hard terrain where we trail ride. Now with

Simple Boots I don't have to worry about cracks at all. I had spent lots of time trying other boots for my horse, but all others seem to have a fault in some way. Some are a pain to put on, some do not provide traction for the hoof mechanism, some do damage to the hooves, etc.—the list goes on! Well, I choose Simple Boots because they are very user-friendly, of course, but more than that, my horse walks out great on trails. No rough terrain bothers him at all, the boots don't slip off the hooves, and they can be fitted so they stay in place on the hoof. Keep up the good work!"

- Nicole Martin and Sky Blue Peppy, Switzerland

68567346R00115

Made in the USA
Columbia, SC
09 August 2019